CONNECTED  MATHEMATICS®3

Additional Practice and Skills Workbook

Grade 6

Glenda Lappan
Elizabeth Difanis Phillips
James T. Fey
Susan N. Friel

PEARSON

Connected Mathematics® was developed at Michigan State University with financial support from the Michigan State University Office of the Provost, Computing and Technology, and the College of Natural Science.

This material is based upon work supported by the National Science Foundation under Grant No. MDR 9150217 and Grant No. ESI 9986372. Opinions expressed are those of the authors and not necessarily those of the Foundation.

As with prior editions of this work, the authors and administration of Michigan State University preserve a tradition of devoting royalties from this publication to support activities sponsored by the MSU Mathematics Enrichment Fund.

13-digit ISBN 978-0-328-90119-7
10-digit ISBN 0-328-90119-9

Table of Contents

Covering and Surrounding

Decimal Operations

Variables and Patterns

Data About Us

Additional Practice

1. For each of the following, use the set of clues to determine the secret number.

   a. Clue 1   The number has two digits.

      Clue 2   The number has 13 as a factor.

      Clue 3   The sum of the digits of the number is 11.

   b. Clue 1   The number is prime.

      Clue 2   The number is less than 19.

      Clue 3   The sum of the digits of the number is greater than 7.

2. The numbers 10, 20, and 30 on the 30-board in the Factor Game all have 10 as a factor. Does *any* number that has 10 as a factor also have 5 as a factor? Explain your reasoning.

3. The numbers 14, 28, and 42 on the 49-board in the Factor Game all have 7 as a factor and also have 2 as a factor. Does *any* number that has 7 as a factor also have 2 as a factor? Explain your reasoning.

Additional Practice (continued)

4. Look carefully at the numbers 1–30 on the 30-board used for playing the Factor Game. Pick the two different numbers on the 30-board that will give you the largest number when you multiply them together, and then answer the following questions.

   a. What two numbers did you pick? What is the product of the two numbers?

   b. Explain why the product of the two numbers you chose is the largest product you can get using two different numbers from the 30-board.

   c. List all the proper factors of the product. Explain how you found the factors.

5. For each of the following, find three different numbers that can be multiplied together so that the given number is the product. Do not use 1 as one of the numbers.

   a. 150   b. 1,000   c. 24   d. 66

Additional Practice (continued)

6. The number sequence 4, 6, 10 is a multiple of the number sequence 2, 3, 5 because the sequence 4, 6, 10 can be found by multiplying all the numbers in the sequence 2, 3, 5 by 2. That is, $4 = 2 \times 2, 6 = 2 \times 3, 10 = 2 \times 5$.

   a. The number sequence 15, 25, 10 is a multiple of what number sequence?

   b. Find two different sequences that are multiples of the number sequence 1, 4, 7.

   c. Given a number sequence, how many different sets of multiples of that sequence do you think there are? Explain your reasoning.

7. For each set of numbers, write as many different multiplication and division statements as you can. For example, if the numbers are 5, 7, 35, you can write:

   $5 \times 7 = 35$ $7 \times 5 = 35$ $35 \div 5 = 7$ $35 \div 7 = 5$

   a. 6, 4, 24   b. 96, 12, 8, 3, 32   c. 6, 27, 108, 12, 4, 18, 9

   d. When is a number called a factor of a number? A divisor of a number?

Additional Practice: Digital Assessments

8. Circle the numbers or equations that make the statement true.

The number $\begin{bmatrix} 2 \\ 7 \\ 9 \\ 95 \\ 178 \\ 188 \end{bmatrix}$ is a multiple of 94 because $\begin{bmatrix} 2 \times 94 = 178 \\ 2 \times 94 = 188 \\ 2 \times 47 = 94 \end{bmatrix}$.

9. Place each number in the correct category.

43   88   99   13   41   71   25   107   49   76

Prime	Composite

10. Using the numbers on the tiles provided below, write the factors of 36.

| 1 | 2 | 3 | 4 | 5 |

| 6 | 9 | 10 | 12 | 36 |

Factors of 36

11. Which of the following numbers are factors of 28? *Select all that apply.*

☐ 4
☐ 6
☐ 7
☐ 12
☐ 56

Skill: Factors, Multiples, and Primes

List all the factors of each number.

1. 12

2. 45

3. 41

4. 54

5. 48

6. 100

7. 117

Skill: Factors, Multiples, and Primes (continued)

Tell whether the second number is a multiple of the first.

8. 2; 71   **9.** 1; 18   **10.** 3; 81   **11.** 4; 74

12. 9; 522   **13.** 8; 508   **14.** 13; 179   **15.** 17; 3,587

Tell whether each number is prime or composite.

16. 53   **17.** 86   **18.** 95   **19.** 17

20. 24   **21.** 27   **22.** 31   **23.** 51

24. 103   **25.** 47   **26.** 93   **27.** 56

28. Make a list of all the prime numbers from 50 through 75.

Additional Practice

1. On Saturdays, the #14 bus makes roundtrips between Susan's school and the mall, and the #11 bus makes roundtrips between the mall and the museum. Next Saturday, Susan wants to take the bus from her school to the museum. A #14 bus leaves Susan's school every 15 minutes, beginning at 7 A.M. It takes the bus 30 minutes to travel between the school and the mall. A #11 bus leaves the mall every 12 minutes, beginning at 7 A.M.

   a. If Susan gets on the #14 at 9:30 A.M., how long will she have to wait at the mall for a #11 bus? Explain your reasoning.

   b. If Susan gets on the #11 bus at the museum and arrives at the mall at 11:48 A.M., how long will she have to wait for the #14 bus? Explain your reasoning.

   c. At what times from 9 A.M. until noon are the #14 and #11 buses at the mall at the same time? Explain your reasoning.

2. Kyong has built two rectangles. Each has a width of 7 tiles.

   a. Each rectangle is made with an even number of tiles that is greater than 40 but less than 60. How many tiles does it take to make each rectangle? Explain your reasoning.

   b. What is the length of each of Kyong's rectangles? Explain your reasoning.

   c. Without changing the number of tiles used to make either rectangle, Kyong rearranges the tiles of each rectangle into different rectangles. What is a possibility for the length and width of each of Kyong's new rectangles? Explain your reasoning.

Additional Practice *(continued)*

3. Jack plays on a basketball team after school (or on the weekend) every third day of the month. He babysits his younger brother after school every seventh day of the month. How many times during a 30-day month, if any, will Jack have a conflict between basketball and babysitting? Explain your reasoning.

4. Suppose you have two different numbers which are both prime.

   a. What is the least common multiple of the numbers? Explain your reasoning.

   b. What is the greatest common factor? Explain your reasoning.

5. Find the least common multiple and the greatest common factor for each pair of numbers:

   a. 8 and 12   **b.** 7 and 15   **c.** 11 and 17   **d.** 36 and 108

   e. For which pairs in parts (a)–(d) is the least common multiple the product of the two numbers? Why is this so? What is special about the numbers in these pairs?

6. Find the greatest common factor of each pair of numbers:

   a. 4 and 12   **b.** 5 and 15   **c.** 10 and 40   **d.** 25 and 75

   e. When is the greatest common factor of two numbers one of the two numbers? Explain your reasoning.

Additional Practice: Digital Assessments

7. Using the numbers provided below, fill in each space to complete the statement. Some numbers may be used more than once.

2   3   4   6   8   10   12   20   48   50   60   120

  a. Greatest common factor of 4 and 8: [   ] ; least common multiple of 4 and 8: [   ]

  b. Greatest common factor of 16 and 24: [   ] ; least common multiple of 16 and 24: [   ]

  c. Greatest common factor of 10 and 60: [   ] ; least common multiple of 10 and 60: [   ]

  d. Greatest common factor of 8 and 30: [   ] ; least common multiple of 8 and 30: [   ]

8. Frank has built two rectangles. Each rectangle has a width of 9 tiles. The rectangles have different lengths. Each rectangle is made with an even number of tiles that is greater than 40 but less than 80. Circle the numbers that make each statement true.

  a. One rectangle was built with $\begin{bmatrix} 36 \\ 46 \\ 54 \\ 61 \end{bmatrix}$ tiles and the other was built with $\begin{bmatrix} 63 \\ 71 \\ 72 \\ 80 \end{bmatrix}$ tiles.

  b. The lengths of the two rectangles are $\begin{bmatrix} 4 \\ 5 \\ 6 \end{bmatrix}$ and $\begin{bmatrix} 7 \\ 8 \\ 9 \end{bmatrix}$ tiles.

Without changing the total number of tiles he has, Frank rearranges the tiles into two different rectangles.

  c. Which of the following could be the dimensions of Frank's new rectangles? *Select all that apply.*

  ☐ 2 by 7 and 7 by 9

  ☐ 6 by 11 and 5 by 12

  ☐ 6 by 7 and 7 by 12

  ☐ 4 by 10 and 6 by 10

  ☐ 7 by 10 and 8 by 7

9. A red bus leaves a theme park every 24 minutes and a blue bus leaves the park every 20 minutes. They both leave the park at noon. When is the next time that both buses will leave the park?

  ○ 12:48 P.M.

  ○ 1:20 P.M.

  ○ 1:34 P.M.

  ○ 1:40 P.M.

  ○ 2:00 P.M.

Skill: Least Common Multiple

List multiples to find the LCM of each set of numbers.

1. 5, 10

2. 2, 3

3. 6, 8

4. 4, 6

5. 8, 10

6. 5, 6

7. 12, 15

8. 8, 12

9. 9, 15

10. 6, 15

11. 6, 9

12. 6, 18

13. 3, 5

14. 4, 5

15. 9, 21

16. 7, 28

17. One radio station broadcasts a weather forecast every 18 minutes and another station broadcasts a commercial every 15 minutes. If the stations broadcast both a weather forecast and a commercial at noon, when is the next time that both will be broadcast at the same time?

Skill: Greatest Common Factor

List the factors to find the GCF of each set of numbers.

1. 8, 12

2. 18, 27

3. 15, 23

4. 17, 34

5. 24, 12

6. 18, 24

7. 5, 25

8. 20, 25

9. 10, 15

10. 25, 75

11. 14, 21

12. 18, 57

13. 32, 24, 40

14. 25, 60, 75

15. 12, 35, 15

16. 15, 35, 20

17. Cameron is making bead necklaces. He has 90 green beads and 108 blue beads. What is the greatest number of identical necklaces he can make if he wants to use all of the beads?

Additional Practice

1. Solve each multiplication maze below. Record your solution for each maze by tracing the path through the maze.

a. **Maze 924**

Enter →

2	3	7	2
6	2	7	11
5	4	9	10

Exit →

b. **Maze 1080**

2	8	6	3
27	5	7	2
2	5	2	9

Exit →

Enter →

c. **Maze 38220**

14	39	70	91
7	2	20	60
42	15	2	2
98	26	13	7

Enter →

Exit →

d. **Maze 210**

Enter →

3	10	3	14
2	3	5	7
35	2	105	2
7	15	6	3

Exit →

2. Use expanded form to write the prime factorization for each number.

   a. 630

   b. 144

   c. 1,011

   d. 133

   e. 23

3. Use exponents to write the prime factorization for each number.

   a. 630

   b. 144

   c. 64

   d. 250

   e. 392

Additional Practice (continued)

4. For each of the pairs of numbers given below, find the greatest common factor and the least common multiple.

   a. 25 and 105   **b.** 27 and 81   **c.** 36 and 63

5. An odd number that is less than 160 has exactly three different prime factors. What is the number? Explain your reasoning.

6. What number has the prime factorization $2^3 \times 3^2 \times 5^2$?

7. a. Name a pair of numbers whose greatest common factor is the same as one of the numbers.

  b. Name another pair of numbers whose greatest common factor is the same as one of the numbers.

  c. Make a conjecture about what must be true about the least common multiple of any number pairs in which one number is the same as the greatest common factor.

Additional Practice (continued)

8. a. Are 45 and 64 relatively prime? Explain your reasoning.

b. Are 25 and 36 relatively prime? Explain your reasoning.

c. Is it possible for two numbers that are both even to be relatively prime? Why or why not?

d. How can you choose one number so that it will be relatively prime to any other number?

9. In the 1,000-locker problem, which students touched the lockers indicated?

a. both lockers 13 and 19

b. lockers 12, 16, and 20

10. In the 1,000-locker problem, what was the last locker touched by the students indicated?

a. both students 20 and 25

b. both students 13 and 19

c. all three students 3, 4, and 5

d. all three students 30, 40, and 50

Additional Practice: Digital Assessments

11. At a store, rolls come in packages of twenty and veggie burgers come in packages of twelve. Determine the least number of packages of each type that you can buy and have no rolls or burgers left over.

Circle the numbers that make the statement true.

You should purchase $\begin{bmatrix} 1 \\ 2 \\ 3 \\ 4 \\ 5 \end{bmatrix}$ packages of rolls

and $\begin{bmatrix} 2 \\ 3 \\ 4 \\ 5 \\ 6 \end{bmatrix}$ packages of veggie burgers.

12. Using the numbers on the tiles provided below, fill in each space to write the prime factorization of the numbers. Tiles may be used more than once.

2	2^2	2^3	2^4

3	5	13	17

a. $60 = \boxed{} \times \boxed{} \times \boxed{}$

b. $136 = \boxed{} \times \boxed{}$

c. $80 = \boxed{} \times \boxed{}$

13. Use the numbers below to find the greatest common factor of each pair of numbers. Write the GCF in the appropriate box.

1   3   4   5   6   8   15   25   27

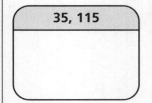   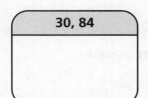   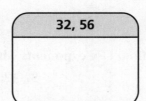   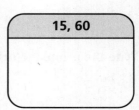

35, 115	30, 84	32, 56	15, 60

14. There are 36 students in a class. Circle the numbers that make each statement true.

a. The class can be divided evenly into $\begin{bmatrix} 2 \\ 3 \\ 4 \\ 6 \end{bmatrix}$ groups with $\begin{bmatrix} 4 \\ 6 \\ 7 \end{bmatrix}$ students in each group.

b. The class can be divided evenly into $\begin{bmatrix} 4 \\ 8 \\ 12 \end{bmatrix}$ groups with $\begin{bmatrix} 2 \\ 3 \\ 8 \end{bmatrix}$ students in each group.

Skill: Prime Factorization

Find the prime factorization of each number.

1. 58

2. 72

3. 40

4. 310

Find the number with the given prime factorization.

5. $2 \times 2 \times 5 \times 7 \times 11$

6. $7 \times 11 \times 13 \times 17$

7. There are 32 students in a class. How many ways can the class be divided into groups with equal numbers of students? What are they?

Write the prime factorization. Use exponents where possible.

8. 78

9. 126

10. 125

11. 90

12. 92

13. 180

Skill: Prime Factorization (continued)

Use prime factorization to find the LCM of each set of numbers.

14. 18, 21   **15.** 15, 21   **16.** 18, 24   **17.** 21, 24

18. At a store, hot dogs come in packages of eight and hot dog buns come in packages of twelve. What is the least number of packages of each type that you can buy and have no hot dogs or buns left over?

Use prime factorization to find the GCF of each set of numbers.

19. 57, 27   **20.** 24, 48   **21.** 56, 35   **22.** 29, 87

23. The GCF of two numbers is 850. Neither number is divisible by the other. What is the smallest that these two numbers could be?

Additional Practice

1. Make a conjecture about whether each result below will be odd or even.
   Support your conjecture.

   a. the sum of two even numbers and one odd number

   b. the sum of two odd numbers and one even number

   c. the sum of three odd numbers

   d. the sum of three even numbers

2. Write expressions for the area of each large rectangle in two different ways.
   Then find the area using each expression.

   a.

   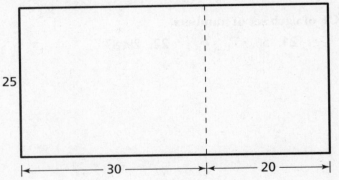

   b.

   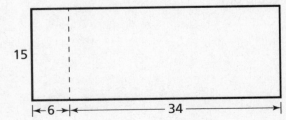

Additional Practice (continued)

3. Find a number to make each statement true.

   a. $25 \times (10 + 7) = (25 \times \square) + (25 \times 7)$

   b. $16 \times (13 + 32) = (\square \times 13) + (\square \times 32)$

   c. $7 \times (92 + 7) = (7 \times 92) + (7 \times \square)$

   d. $74 \times (19 + 19) = (74 \times \square) + (74 \times 19)$

   e. $8(\square + 7) = 96$

   f. $\square(21) + \square(4) = 300$

   g. $12(\square - 21) = 144$

Additional Practice (continued)

4. Insert parentheses and/or addition signs to make each equation true.

   a. 6   3   2   5   = 16

   b. 6   3   2   5   = 23

   c. 6   3   2   5   = 35

   d. 6   3   2   5   = 36

5. Identify the error. Then find the correct solution.

   $4 + 4(8 - 6)$

   $= 8(8 - 6)$

   $= 64 - 48$

   $= 16$

Additional Practice (continued)

Decide on the operation(s) needed to solve the problem. Write a mathematical sentence, solve the problem, and explain your reasoning.

6. A small business employs 26 people for 5 days each week. Of the employees, 8 are paid $128 per day and the rest are paid $92 per day. How much does the business pay out to employees in one week?

7. Tickets to a school play cost $2.50 for a student and $5.00 for an adult. What is the total ticket sales if 50 student tickets and 75 adult tickets are sold?

8. Layne ran 3 miles a day for her first week of track practice. For the next two weeks, she ran 5 miles each day. How many miles did Layne run in her first three weeks of practice, assuming she ran 7 days a week?

9. Manny has $24 at the beginning of the day. He buys 3 drinks that each cost $3. He also buys 2 sandwiches, which are $5 each. Does Manny have any money left? If so, how much?

10. Hannah is 3 years older than her sister Anji. Their brother Tomas is 4 years younger than Hannah. How does Anji's age relate to Tomas' age?

Additional Practice: Digital Assessments

11. Which of the following expressions represent the area of the larger rectangle? *Select all that apply.*

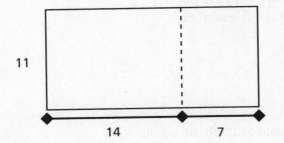

- ☐ $11 \times (14 + 7)$
- ☐ $2 \times 21 + 2 \times 11$
- ☐ $11 \times 14 \times 7$
- ☐ $11 \times 14 + 11 \times 7$
- ☐ 11×21

12. Jenna ran 3 miles a day for her first week of marathon training. For the next two weeks, she ran 4 miles each day. Assume Jenna ran 7 days a week.

Use the numbers and symbols provided to complete parts (a) and (b). Numbers and symbols may be used more than once.

a. Write a mathematical expression to represent the number of miles Jenna ran in her first 3 weeks of training.

b. Evaluate your expression to find the total number of miles Jenna ran.

13. Complete the statements below by circling the expressions or numbers that make each statement true.

$$6 \times (5 \times 5 - 1) - 4$$

To evaluate the expression above using the order of operations, first compute $\begin{bmatrix} 5 \times 5 \\ 5 - 1 \end{bmatrix}$.

Next compute $\begin{bmatrix} 5 \times 4 \\ 6 \times 5 \\ 25 - 1 \end{bmatrix}$.

The expression $6 \times (5 \times 5 - 1) - 4$ simplifies to $\begin{bmatrix} 116 \\ 140 \\ 149 \end{bmatrix}$.

Skill: Areas of Rectangles

Write expressions for the area of each large rectangle in two different ways.
Then find the area using each expression.

1.
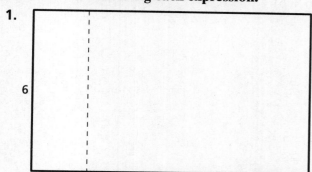

2.
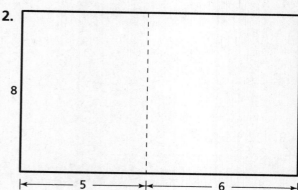

3.
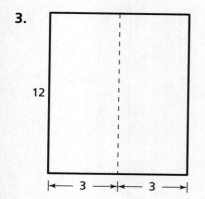

4.
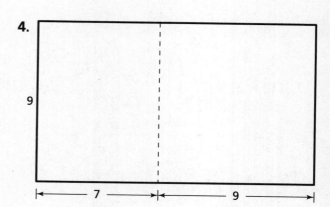

Skill: Order of Operations

Use the Order of Operations to simplify each expression. Show your work.

1. $8 \div 1 + 7$

2. $9(6 + 6)$

3. $(12 - 3) \div 3$

4. $12 - 3 \div 3$

5. $8 \times (4 \times 4 - 6) - 8$

6. $8 \times 4 \times 4 - 6 - 8$

7. $112 - 21 \div 7$

8. $(112 - 21) \div 7$

9. $25 \times (10 - 7)$

10. $25 \times 10 - 7$

11. $(5 \times 3 + 1 - 6) \div 2$

12. $5 \times 3 + 1 - 6 \div 2$

Additional Practice

1. a. For each of the fraction strips below, write a fraction that expresses how much of the strip is shaded.

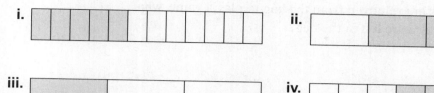

b. For each of the six fraction strips above, write a fraction that expresses how much of the strip is not shaded.

c. For each fraction strip, how is the fraction you wrote for the shaded part related to the fraction you wrote for the unshaded part? Explain your reasoning.

2. The drawing shows the controls on a sound system. Use the drawing to answer each question.

a. What fraction of the total volume is the sound system playing?

b. What fraction of the total bass output is the sound system playing?

c. Write the ratio of the volume level that is playing to the highest possible volume.

d. Write the ratio of the total bass ouput to the bass level that is playing.

e. If Wilbur doubles the bass output that is playing now, what fraction of the total bass output will be the new bass output? Explain your reasoning.

Additional Practice (continued)

3. A bag contains 24 marbles. (**Note:** You may want to use 24 cubes, chips, marbles, or other objects to help you solve this problem.)

   a. If 16 of the marbles are removed from the bag to play a game, what fraction of the marbles are left in the bag?

   b. What is the ratio of the marbles that were removed to the marbles that are left in the bag?

4. Joey's father stops at the gas station to buy gas. The car has a 16-gallon tank, and the fuel gauge says there is $\frac{3}{8}$ of a tank of gas.

   a. How many gallons of gas are in the tank?

   b. If Joey's father buys 6 gallons of gas, what fraction of the tank will the car's fuel gauge read?

   c. What fraction of the gas tank is empty after Joey's father puts 6 gallons of gas in the tank?

Additional Practice (continued)

5. For parts (a)–(b), use fraction strips or some other method to name the point with a fraction.

a.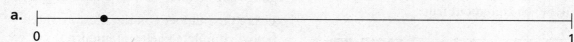

b.

6. For parts (a)–(c), shade each grid to represent the given fraction.

a. Represent the fraction $\frac{4}{5}$ on each grid. Then name each equivalent fraction.

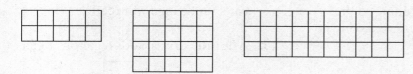

b. Represent the fraction $\frac{3}{7}$ on each grid. Then name each equivalent fraction.

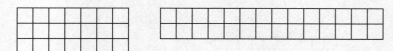

c. Represent the fraction $\frac{1}{6}$ on each grid. Then name each equivalent fraction.

7. Tony is driving from Alma, Michigan to Elizabeth City, North Carolina. The drive covers a total distance of 1,100 miles. Tony's car can travel 400 miles on a full tank of gas. How many tanks of gas will Tony's car need for the entire trip? Explain your reasoning.

Additional Practice: Digital Assessments

8. The image below shows the controls on a sound system. Circle the numbers that make each statement true.

a. The treble playing is $\begin{bmatrix} \frac{1}{5} \\ \frac{1}{2} \\ \frac{3}{5} \end{bmatrix}$ of the total treble.

b. The ratio of the total volume to the volume the sound system is playing is $\begin{bmatrix} 3 \text{ to } 4 \\ 4 \text{ to } 3 \\ 3 \text{ to } 1 \end{bmatrix}$.

9. A car has a 12-gallon tank, and the fuel gauge shows there is $\frac{1}{4}$ of a tank of gas. Using the numbers on the tiles provided below, complete each statement.

3	4	5	6

$\frac{1}{4}$	$\frac{1}{3}$	$\frac{1}{2}$	$\frac{2}{3}$	$\frac{3}{4}$

a. There are [ ] gallons of gas in the tank.

b. After the driver adds 6 gallons of gas, the car's fuel gauge will read [ ].

c. After the driver adds 6 gallons of gas, the gas tank will be [ ] empty.

10. Shade the grid to show $\frac{4}{5}$.

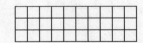

11. Which of the following fractions are equivalent to the amount of the grid that is shaded?

Select all that apply.

☐ $\frac{3}{12}$

☐ $\frac{1}{5}$

☐ $\frac{15}{20}$

☐ $\frac{1}{4}$

Additional Practice

A deli cook makes long submarine sandwiches that are meant to be shared. She cuts the sandwiches into shorter sections. In exercises 1–4, find the fraction of a submarine sandwich each person gets.

1. a. Show how eight sections of sandwich can be shared equally by six people.

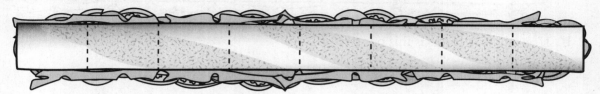

   b. How many sections does each person get?

2. a. Show how six sections of sandwich can be shared equally by eight people.

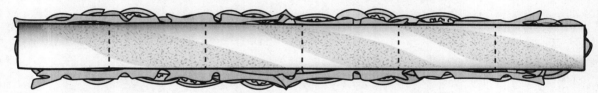

   b. How many sections are there for each person?

3. a. Show how five sections of sandwich can be shared equally by four people.

   b. How many sections does each person get?

Additional Practice (continued)

4. a. Show how four sections of sandwich can be shared equally by five people.

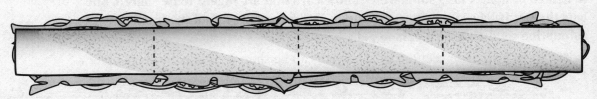

  b. How many sections is this per person?

5. Each week four teachers share a 60-minute lunch duty equally. They also share five 20-minute after-school duties equally.

  a. Write a rate that compares the number of minutes of weekly lunch duty to the number of teachers.

  b. Write a unit rate for the number of minutes of weekly after-school duty for each teacher.

6. A group of students is working in a booth to support their community center. The amount of time each student works is in a ratio according to their ages.

  a. Abby is 16 years old. Kiaya is 12 years old. If Abby works 120 minutes, how many minutes does Kiaya work? How long do they work altogether?

Additional Practice (continued)

b. Jacob is 14 years old. Matthew is 10 years old. They work 120 minutes altogether. How many minutes does each boy work?

c. Hannah and Michael work together. Hannah works 160 minutes. Michael works 100 minutes. How old could each of them be?

7. A group of friends is working together on a building project. The number of hours each person works as a team depends on their number of years of experience.

a. Lauren has 8 years of experience. Kim has 2 years of experience. If Lauren works for 48 hours, how many hours does Kim work? How long do they work altogether?

b. James has 12 years of experience. Becky has 6 years of experience. They work 108 hours altogether. How many hours does each person work?

c. Kelly and Mitchell work together. Kelly works 9 hours. Mitchell works 15 hours. How many years of experience could each person have?

Investigation 2

Additional Practice *(continued)*

8. Use rate tables to find how much each person makes in 1 hour and how long each person has to work to make $1.

a. Paula remembers that she worked 20 hours and made $80.

Hours	1	10	20		30	
Pay ($)			80	100		1

b. Ben works 15 hours and is paid $75.

Hours	1		15	30		
Pay ($)		25	75		190	1

c. Patrick is paid $12 for 3 hours of work.

Hours	1	3		36		
Pay ($)		12	60		192	1

d. Kayla is paid $72 for 9 hours of work.

Hours	1	4	9		16	
Pay ($)			72	88		1

9. Bill measures the lengths of six boards he finds in his garage. Name two boards he could be comparing for each ratio given.

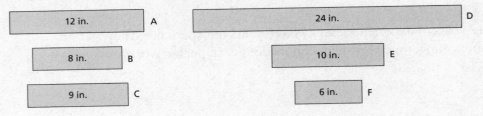

a. The ratio of lengths is 2 : 1.   Board _____ to Board _____

b. The ratio of lengths is 4 : 1.   Board _____ to Board _____

c. The ratio of lengths is 3 : 4.   Board _____ to Board _____

d. The ratio of lengths is 2 : 3.   Board _____ to Board _____

Additional Practice (continued)

10. George is planning his road trip. He uses a vertical rate table.

   a. Complete the rate table for the gas his car will use.

George's Car

Gallons of Gas	Miles
1	36
2	
3	
4	
5	
6	

   b. How many gallons of gas will he use if he drives 432 miles?

   c. How many miles can he go if he uses 8 gallons of gas?

11. George uses another vertical rate table to keep track of his gasoline expenses.

   a. Complete the rate table for the cost of the gas he will purchase.

Gas Purchases

Gallons of Gas	Cost ($)
6	24
5	
4	
3	
2	
1	

   b. What is the unit rate comparing the number of dollars to the gallons of gas?

   c. What is the unit rate comparing the gallons of gas to the cost in dollars?

Additional Practice: Digital Assessments

12. Which of the following is equivalent to the ratio 3 to 7? *Select all that apply.*

☐ $\frac{6}{14}$

☐ $\frac{7}{3}$

☐ 21:56

☐ $\frac{24}{56}$

☐ 60 for every 140

13. Mari works 25 hours and makes $200. Complete the rate table using the numbers on the tiles.

| 5 | 8 | 12 | 15 | 18 |

| 40 | 42 | 64 | $\frac{1}{5}$ | $\frac{1}{8}$ |

Hours	Pay ($)
1	8
5	
	120
25	200
	1

14. Circle the correct unit rate for each situation.

a. Sandi drives 420 miles in 7 hours.

$\begin{bmatrix} \frac{1}{16} \\ 55 \\ 60 \\ 2940 \end{bmatrix}$ miles per hour

b. Four bags of rice cost $7.20.

$\begin{bmatrix} \$0.80 \\ \$1.80 \\ \$3.60 \\ \$28.80 \end{bmatrix}$ per bag

c. Joe needs 0.25 hour to tie 3 decorative bows.

$\begin{bmatrix} \frac{1}{12} \\ \frac{1}{4} \\ 6 \\ 12 \end{bmatrix}$ bows per hour

Skill: Ratios and Rates

Write two ratios that are equivalent to the given ratio.

1. $1:3$

2. 2 for every 5

3. 5 to 8

4. 4 for every 9

5. 35 for every 50

6. $90:180$

7. $150:180$

8. 56 to 84

9. 25 to 75

10. $42:126$

Skill: Ratios and Rates (continued)

Find the unit rate for each situation.

11. Trisha drives 200 miles in 4 hours.

12. Cans of baked beans cost $2.40 for 3 cans.

13. Derek put 26 batteries into 13 smoke detectors.

14. Crystal spent $83.70 on 6 tickets to the theater.

15. Garrett needs 0.5 hour to install 4 new tires.

16. There are 630 calories in 6 bananas.

Additional Practice

1. The diagram at the right is a hundredths grid. A shaded hundredths grid represents the number 1. Use the grid to answer each of the following questions and write each answer in both decimal and fraction form.

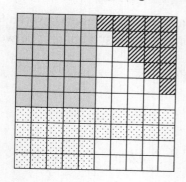

   a. What portion of the grid is shaded gray?

   b. What portion of the grid is striped?

   c. What portion of the grid is dotted?

   d. What portion of the grid is blank?

2. For each pair of numbers, insert a less-than symbol (<), a greater-than symbol (>), or an equals symbol (=) between the numbers to make a true statement.

   a. 0.305   0.35

   b. 0.123   0.1002

   c. 0.25   0.25000

   d. 0.25   0.025

   e. 3.45   3.045

   f. 12.03   12.30

Additional Practice (continued)

3. For each pair of numbers, insert a less-than symbol (<), greater-than symbol
(>), or an equals symbol (=) between the numbers to make a true statement.

a. 2.5 $2\frac{2}{5}$

b. 0.65 $\frac{2}{3}$

c. 0.8 $\frac{4}{7}$

d. $\frac{5}{8}$ 0.625

e. 0.3 $\frac{3}{7}$

f. 2.1 $1\frac{9}{10}$

g. $\frac{11}{12}$ $\frac{11}{11}$

h. $\frac{3}{6}$ 0.5

i. 9 $8\frac{8}{10}$

4. In each number line, two of the marks are labeled. Label the unlabeled marks
with decimal numbers.

a.

0.3   0.6

b.

0.11   0.13

c.

0.03   0.12

d.

                               0.5   0.75

Additional Practice (continued)

5. Name three fractions that are equivalent to each decimal below.

    a. 0.60   **b.** 1.7   **c.** 0.05   **d.** 2.3   **e.** 0.15   **f.** 0.625

6. Name a decimal that is equivalent to each fraction below.

    a. $\frac{1}{2}$ **b.** $\frac{3}{15}$ **c.** $\frac{7}{4}$ **d.** $\frac{3}{8}$ **e.** $\frac{111}{20}$ **f.** $\frac{18}{24}$

7. Sarah can jog at a steady pace of 4.75 miles per hour, and Tony can jog at a steady pace of 4.25 miles per hour.

    a. How many miles can Sarah jog in 30 minutes? Explain your reasoning.

    b. How many miles can Tony jog in 30 minutes?

    c. If Sarah and Tony jog for 45 minutes, how much farther will Sarah go than Tony? Explain your reasoning.

Additional Practice (continued)

8. Each square on the grid represents $\frac{1}{5}$.

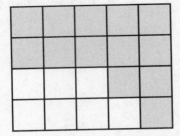

    a. What whole number is represented by the whole grid?

    b. What decimal is represented by the shaded region of the grid?

9. Each square on the grid represents 0.25.

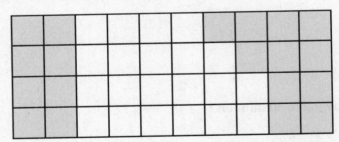

    a. What whole number is represented by the whole grid?

    b. What fraction is represented by the shaded region of the grid?

Additional Practice *(continued)*

10. Paul claims that the fraction $\frac{1}{3}$ is a good estimate for the decimal 0.3.

    a. Do you agree or disagree with Paul's claim? Explain your reasoning.

    b. Is Paul's estimate less than, greater than, or equal to 0.3? Explain your reasoning.

11. Locate and label the points representing $-\frac{1}{2}, 1\frac{1}{4}, -2\frac{3}{4}, \frac{5}{2}$.

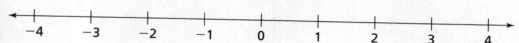

12. Explain what the negative number means in each situation.

    a. The elevation of a diver is ⁻120 meters.

    b. A business had an income of ⁻$1,200 for one day.

    c. The temperature outside is ⁻7° Fahrenheit.

    d. A song moved ⁻6 positions on the music chart.

Additional Practice (continued)

13. Find a rational number between each pair of numbers.

   a. $\frac{1}{3}$ and $\frac{2}{5}$

   b. $-\frac{3}{8}$ and $-\frac{3}{4}$

   c. -0.4 and -0.6

   d. 0.5 and 0.6

14. Find the absolute value of each number.

   a. -0.2

   b. 2.84

   c. $\frac{1}{3}$

   d. $-\frac{5}{6}$

15. Find the opposite of each number.

   a. -3.4

   b. $-\frac{3}{7}$

   c. $\frac{5}{9}$

   d. 0.6

16. Order each set of rational numbers from least to greatest.

   a. $2.1, -0.3, 0.261, -2.56$

   b. $\frac{4}{3}, \frac{1}{3}, -\frac{2}{3}, -3$

Additional Practice: Digital Assessments

17. Circle the correct symbols to make each statement true.

a. 0.48 $\begin{bmatrix} < \\ > \\ = \end{bmatrix}$ 0.408

b. $\frac{2}{7}$ $\begin{bmatrix} < \\ > \\ = \end{bmatrix}$ 0.3

c. $\frac{5}{6}$ $\begin{bmatrix} < \\ > \\ = \end{bmatrix}$ $\frac{5}{5}$

d. 0.78 $\begin{bmatrix} < \\ > \\ = \end{bmatrix}$ 0.7800

e. 1.26 $\begin{bmatrix} < \\ > \\ = \end{bmatrix}$ 1.026

18. Each grid represents 1. Below each grid, use the values from the tiles to write the fraction and decimal modeled by the shaded areas.

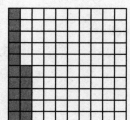

| 0.15 | 0.60 | 0.015 | 0.06 |

| $\frac{3}{5}$ | $\frac{3}{20}$ | $\frac{3}{25}$ | $\frac{3}{50}$ |

19. Shade and label the points listed below on the number line.

$1\frac{1}{4}$, 0.25, $-\frac{3}{2}$, -1.75

Skill: Fractions and Decimals

Each grid represents 1. What fraction and decimal are modeled by the shaded area?

1. 　　　　**2.** 　　　　**3.**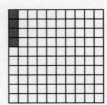

Write each decimal as a fraction.

4. 0.6　　　　**5.** 1.25　　　　**6.** 0.74　　　　**7.** 0.29

8. 0.635　　　　**9.** 0.8　　　　**10.** 0.95　　　　**11.** 0.645

Write each fraction as a decimal.

12. $\frac{9}{100}$　　　　**13.** $\frac{7}{25}$　　　　**14.** $\frac{3}{50}$　　　　**15.** $\frac{1}{125}$

Write each of the decimal numbers in words.

16. 12.873

17. 8.0552

18. 0.00065

Skill: Comparing and Ordering Decimals

Insert <, >, or = in each box to make a true statement.

1. 0.62 ☐ 0.618

2. 9.8 ☐ 9.80

3. 1.006 ☐ 1.02

4. −41.3 ☐ −41.03

5. 2.01 ☐ 2.011

6. −5.079 ☐ −5.08

7. 15.8 ☐ 15.800

8. 7.98 ☐ 7.89

9. 5.693 ☐ 5.299

Order each set of decimals on a number line.

10. 0.2, 0.6, 0.5

11. 0.26, 0.3, 0.5, 0.59, 0.7

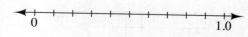 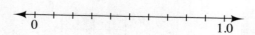

12. Three points are graphed on the number line below. Write statements comparing 0.3 to 0.5 and 0.5 to 0.7.

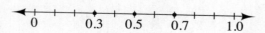

13. Models for three decimals are shown below.

   a. Write decimal names that each shaded part represents.

   b. Rewrite the decimals in order from least to greatest.

Additional Practice

Comparing Bits and Pieces

1. For each of the grids given below, express the shaded region of the grid as a ratio, a fraction, and a percent.

a.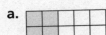

b.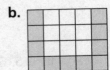

c.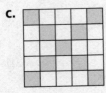

d.

e.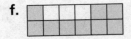

f.

Additional Practice (continued)

2. Angie and Jim conducted a survey of their sixth-grade classmates in their mathematics class. They found out the following information:

- 70% of the students in the class do homework three or more nights each week.

- Of the students who do homework three or more nights each week, half do homework five nights each week.

a. What percentage of the students in the class do homework two nights or less each week? Explain your reasoning.

b. What fraction of the students in the class do homework five nights each week? Explain your reasoning.

c. What percentage of students in the class do homework three or four nights a week? Explain your reasoning.

d. From the information provided, can you tell how many students are in the class? Explain why or why not.

Additional Practice (continued)

3. In a class of 24 sixth-graders, 25% walk to school, $\frac{1}{8}$ ride bicycles to school, $\frac{1}{3}$ take the bus to school, and the remainder of the class are driven to school by their parents or guardians.

   a. How many students in the class walk to school? Explain your reasoning.

   b. How many students in the class ride bicycles to school? Explain your reasoning.

   c. How many students in the class take the bus to school?

   d. What is the ratio of students who are driven to class by their parent or guardian to students in the class?

   e. What percentage of the students in the class walk, ride bicycles or the bus, or are driven to school by a parent or guardian? Explain your reasoning.

Additional Practice (continued)

4. Express the shaded region of each drawing as a fraction, a decimal, and as a percent.

a.

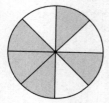

b.

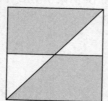

c.

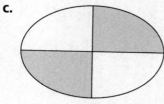

d.

Additional Practice (continued)

5. In one competition, the archery team had to shoot at targets from three different distances: 10 m, 20 m, and 30 m. The number of hits and the number of shots for each distance are given below. Write their score for each round as a fraction, a decimal, and a percent.

   a. at 10 m: 42 hits out of 50 shots

   b. at 20 m: 37 hits out of 50 shots

   c. at 30 m: 18 hits out of 50 shots

6. Fill in the missing parts of the table.

Fraction	Decimal	Percent
$\frac{3}{8}$		
	0.88	
		35%
$1\frac{1}{4}$		
	0.625	
		275%

Additional Practice: Digital Assessments

7. Charlotte conducted a survey with her classmates about the number of pets in each household.

- 60% of the students in the class said they had 2 or more pets.
- Of the students who said they had 2 or more pets, one-third of them said they had 3 or more pets.

Circle the numbers that make each statement true.

a. The percentage of students in the class that have fewer than 2 pets is $\begin{bmatrix} 60\% \\ 40\% \\ 33\% \\ 20\% \end{bmatrix}$.

b. The fraction of the students in the class that have 3 or more pets is $\begin{bmatrix} \frac{1}{5} \\ \frac{1}{3} \\ \frac{1}{2} \end{bmatrix}$.

8. In a class of 30 students, 40% participate in a sports activity after school, $\frac{1}{3}$ participate in an arts-based activity after school, $\frac{1}{5}$ participate in a volunteer activity after school, and the remainder of the students do not participate in an after-school activity. Which of the following statements are true? *Select all that apply.*

☐ Eight students participate in a sports activity after school.

☐ Six students participate in a volunteer activity after school.

☐ More students participate in an arts-based activity than a volunteer activity after school.

☐ The fraction of the students that do not participate in an after-school activity is $\frac{1}{15}$.

☐ The ratio of students that participate in an arts-based activity to the students that participate in a volunteer activity is 3:5.

Skill: Percents

Shade each grid to represent each of the following percents.

1. 53%

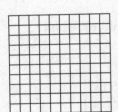

2. 23%

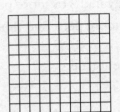

3. 71%

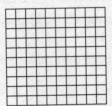

Write a percent for each shaded figure.

4.

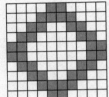

5.

6.

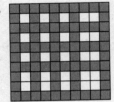

The table shows the fraction of students who participated in extracurricular activities from 1965 to 2000. For Exercises 7–14, complete the table by writing each fraction as a percent.

Students' Extracurricular Choices

Year	1965	1970	1975	1980	1985	1990	1995	2000
Student participation (fraction)	$\frac{3}{4}$	$\frac{8}{10}$	$\frac{17}{20}$	$\frac{39}{50}$	$\frac{21}{25}$	$\frac{19}{25}$	$\frac{87}{100}$	$\frac{9}{10}$
Student participation (percent)	**7.**	**8.**	**9.**	**10.**	**11.**	**12.**	**13.**	**14.**

Write each fraction as a percent.

15. $\frac{4}{5}$

16. $\frac{3}{5}$

17. $\frac{9}{10}$

18. $\frac{3}{10}$

19. $\frac{6}{25}$

20. $\frac{7}{100}$

21. $\frac{9}{50}$

22. $\frac{9}{25}$

23. $\frac{2}{5}$

24. $\frac{7}{10}$

25. $\frac{4}{25}$

26. $\frac{16}{25}$

Skill: Percents, Fractions, and Decimals

Write each percent as a decimal and as a fraction.

1. 46%   **2.** 17%   **3.** 90%   **4.** 5%

Write each decimal as a percent and as a fraction.

5. 0.02   **6.** 0.45   **7.** 0.4   **8.** 0.92

Write each fraction as a decimal and as a percent.

9. $\frac{3}{5}$ **10.** $\frac{7}{10}$ **11.** $\frac{13}{25}$ **12.** $\frac{17}{20}$

13. Write each fraction or decimal as a percent. Write the percent (without the percent sign) in the puzzle.

ACROSS

1. $\frac{3}{5}$

2. $\frac{1}{5}$

3. 0.55

5. 0.23

6. $\frac{7}{20}$

7. 0.17

9. 0.4

10. $\frac{9}{25}$

DOWN

1. $\frac{13}{20}$

2. 0.25

3. $\frac{1}{2}$

4. $\frac{3}{20}$

5. 0.24

6. $\frac{3}{10}$

7. 0.1

8. $\frac{4}{25}$

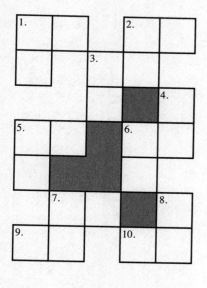

Additional Practice

1. Suppose you roll a red number cube and a green number cube and form a fraction with the number on the red number cube as the numerator and the number on the green number cube as the denominator.

   a. List all the possible fractions.

   b. List all the fractions that are between $\frac{2}{3}$ and $1\frac{1}{2}$.

   c. List all the fractions that are between $2\frac{1}{3}$ and $3\frac{2}{3}$.

2. For each part, state whether the sum of the fractions is less than, greater than, or equal to 1. Explain your thinking.

   a. $\frac{3}{8} + \frac{2}{5}$

   b. $\frac{5}{10} + \frac{3}{4}$

   c. $\frac{3}{12} + \frac{3}{6}$

   d. $\frac{1}{2} + \frac{4}{8}$

Additional Practice (continued)

e. $\frac{4}{7} + \frac{7}{12}$

f. $\frac{4}{3} + \frac{1}{100}$

g. $\frac{1}{4} + \frac{2}{3}$

h. $\frac{9}{20} + \frac{5}{11}$

3. "Close to One" is a game that uses the "Getting Close" game cards that show fractions less than 1. The object of "Close to One" is to estimate a sum of two fractions that is as close to 1 as possible without exceeding 1. On each turn, the player draws one card. This is the starting value. Then, the player draws three more cards and chooses the one that will make the sum as close to 1 as possible without exceeding 1.

In each sample turn below, the starting value is followed by the value of three game cards. Choose the fraction that will make the sum as close to 1 as possible without exceeding 1. Explain the reasoning for your choice.

a. $\frac{1}{3}$ $\frac{1}{8}, \frac{1}{4}, \frac{1}{2}$

b. $\frac{3}{4}$ $\frac{1}{8}, \frac{1}{3}, \frac{1}{2}$

c. $\frac{2}{5}$ $\frac{1}{4}, \frac{1}{2}, \frac{3}{4}$

d. $\frac{9}{10}$ $\frac{7}{10}, \frac{3}{4}, \frac{2}{3}$

e. $\frac{1}{10}$ $\frac{1}{8}, \frac{1}{5}, \frac{1}{4}$

f. $\frac{3}{8}$ $\frac{4}{9}, \frac{5}{6}, \frac{9}{10}$

Additional Practice (continued)

4. For each set of fractions, list all the possible pairs whose sum is between 1 and $1\frac{1}{2}$.

   a. $\frac{1}{2}, \frac{3}{4}, \frac{7}{8}$

   b. $\frac{1}{3}, \frac{9}{10}, \frac{6}{5}$

   c. $\frac{3}{4}, \frac{7}{8}, \frac{9}{10}$

   d. $\frac{1}{4}, \frac{1}{2}, \frac{3}{5}$

   e. $\frac{1}{10}, \frac{2}{3}, \frac{5}{4}$

   f. $\frac{1}{2}, \frac{3}{5}, \frac{7}{10}$

5. Rosa and Tony need to estimate how much it will cost to purchase the following supplies for their class project.

   4 pieces of posterboard at $2.89 each

   1 bottle of glue at $1.19

   2 booklets of construction paper at $4.99 each

   2 pairs of scissors at $0.59 each

   a. Estimate the cost of the supplies that Rosa and Tony need to buy.

   b. In this situation, would it be better to overestimate or underestimate? Explain.

Additional Practice (continued)

6. Jack and Helen are making cookies. The recipe says to combine $\frac{1}{2}$ cup of butter with $\frac{3}{4}$ cup chocolate chips and $\frac{3}{8}$ cup chopped nuts.

   a. When these three ingredients are mixed together, how many cups of the mixture will Jake and Helen have? Show your work.

   b. Jack and Helen decide to triple the recipe.
      i. How many cups of butter will be needed?

      ii. How many cups of chocolate chips will be needed?

      iii. How many cups of chopped nuts will be needed?

   c. When the ingredients for the tripled recipe are combined, how many cups of the mixture will Jack and Helen have?

Additional Practice *(continued)*

7. Mr. Larson is planning the seating for a school recital. He needs to reserve $\frac{1}{3}$ of the seats for students and $\frac{1}{6}$ of the seats for parents.

   a. After reserving seats for students and parents, what fraction of the seats in the auditorium are left?

   b. Mr. Larson's principal tells him that he also needs to reserve $\frac{1}{8}$ of the seats for teachers and school officials. The remainder can be used for open seating. What fraction of the seats are now left for open seating?

   c. Later, Mr. Larson's principal says he should reserve $\frac{1}{4}$ of the seats for students from other middle schools. Are there enough seats left? If not, explain why not; otherwise, state what fraction of the seats will be available for open seating.

Additional Practice (continued)

8. The shaded region represents one whole unit.

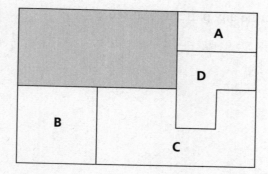

a. What fraction of the whole is each of the other four regions A, B, C, D?

b. Based on your answers to part (a), find the area of each of the following:

i. region A + region B   **ii.** region C + region D

iii. region B − region D   **iv.** region C − region A

c. If the entire outer rectangle is considered the whole, what fraction of the whole would the shaded gray area be? Explain your reasoning.

Additional Practice (continued)

9. Find each sum. Describe any patterns you see.

a. $\frac{1}{2} + \frac{1}{3}$

b. $\frac{1}{3} + \frac{1}{4}$

c. $\frac{1}{4} + \frac{1}{5}$

d. $\frac{1}{5} + \frac{1}{6}$

e. $\frac{1}{6} + \frac{1}{7}$

f. $\frac{1}{7} + \frac{1}{8}$

Additional Practice: Digital Assessments

10. Circle the number that makes each statement true.

a. $\dfrac{1}{6} + \dfrac{2}{3} = \begin{bmatrix} \dfrac{1}{3} \\ \dfrac{5}{6} \\ \dfrac{7}{6} \end{bmatrix}$

b. $5 - 2\dfrac{2}{3} = \begin{bmatrix} 2\dfrac{1}{3} \\ 3\dfrac{2}{3} \\ 4\dfrac{1}{3} \end{bmatrix}$

11. To follow a recipe, Jared has to mix the following liquids: $\dfrac{3}{4}$ cup of water, $\dfrac{1}{8}$ cup of coconut oil, and $\dfrac{3}{8}$ cup of eggs. Which represent how many cups of liquid are in the mixture? *Select all that apply.*

☐ $\dfrac{7}{20}$

☐ $\dfrac{7}{8}$

☐ $\dfrac{5}{4}$

☐ $1\dfrac{1}{4}$

☐ $1\dfrac{1}{2}$

12. Write each expression in the box with the correct category.

$$\dfrac{3}{10} + \dfrac{1}{2} \qquad \dfrac{2}{5} + \dfrac{2}{7} \qquad \dfrac{1}{2} + \dfrac{3}{5}$$

$$\dfrac{1}{6} + \dfrac{3}{4} \qquad \dfrac{2}{7} + \dfrac{2}{9} \qquad \dfrac{1}{4} + \dfrac{5}{6}$$

Sum Greater than 1	Sum Less than 1

Skill: Estimating With Fractions

Write the fraction shown by each model. Then determine whether the number is closest to $0, \frac{1}{2}$, or 1.

1.

2.

Estimate each sum. Use the benchmarks $0, \frac{1}{2}$, and 1.

3. $\frac{5}{16} + \frac{5}{8}$

4. $\frac{10}{12} + \frac{4}{5}$

5. $\frac{1}{10} + \frac{1}{2}$

6. $\frac{3}{4} + \frac{3}{8}$

7. $\frac{1}{12} + \frac{6}{11}$

8. $\frac{8}{14} + \frac{4}{7}$

9. $\frac{1}{6} + \frac{5}{8}$

10. $\frac{1}{10} + \frac{5}{6}$

11. $\frac{9}{10} + \frac{7}{8}$

12. $\frac{1}{12} + \frac{9}{10}$

13. $\frac{15}{16} + \frac{11}{12}$

14. $\frac{1}{8} + \frac{9}{10}$

15. Name three fractions whose benchmark is $\frac{1}{2}$.

16. Name three fractions whose benchmark is 1.

Skill: Estimating With Mixed Numbers

Estimate each sum.

1. $2\frac{1}{6} + 7\frac{1}{9}$ **2.** $4\frac{7}{8} + 8\frac{1}{5}$ **3.** $2\frac{7}{9} + 4\frac{1}{8}$ **4.** $14\frac{3}{4} + 9\frac{7}{8}$

5. $6\frac{7}{8} + \frac{11}{12}$ **6.** $1\frac{1}{8} + 1\frac{1}{5}$ **7.** $2\frac{1}{6} + 1\frac{9}{10}$ **8.** $4\frac{9}{10} + 4\frac{7}{8}$

9. $5\frac{6}{7} + \frac{2}{3}$ **10.** $\frac{1}{7} + 2\frac{7}{8}$ **11.** $2\frac{4}{5} + 1\frac{5}{8}$ **12.** $\frac{2}{13} + 3\frac{1}{18}$

13. $42\frac{1}{6} + 6\frac{1}{16}$ **14.** $6\frac{2}{15} + 1\frac{3}{4}$ **15.** $19\frac{5}{6} + 20\frac{1}{12}$ **16.** $2\frac{1}{4} + 3\frac{15}{16}$

17. $\frac{2}{9} + 2\frac{7}{8}$ **18.** $7\frac{1}{8} + 2\frac{3}{11}$ **19.** $3\frac{4}{5} + 2\frac{1}{8}$ **20.** $\frac{3}{5} + \frac{7}{8}$

21. Julia bought stock at $28\frac{1}{8}$ per share. The value of each share increased by $6\frac{5}{8}$. How much is each share of stock now worth?

Skill: Adding and Subtracting Fractions

Find each sum or difference.

1. $\frac{1}{4} + \frac{2}{4}$

2. $\frac{7}{10} - \frac{4}{10}$

3. $\frac{5}{8} - \frac{3}{8}$

4. $\frac{1}{8} + \frac{5}{8}$

5. $\frac{5}{8} + \frac{2}{8}$

6. $\frac{3}{10} + \frac{6}{10}$

7. $\frac{2}{5} - \frac{1}{10}$

8. $\frac{5}{8} - \frac{1}{4}$

9. $\frac{3}{10} + \frac{4}{5}$

10. $\frac{11}{16} + \frac{5}{8}$

11. $\frac{2}{3} - \frac{1}{6}$

12. $\frac{3}{5} + \frac{7}{10}$

Skill: Adding and Subtracting Fractions (continued)

13. What is the total amount of sugar in the recipe at the right?

Martha's Cookie Recipe
1 cup shortening
2 eggs
$\frac{1}{4}$ cup white sugar
$\frac{1}{4}$ cup brown sugar
$1\frac{1}{2}$ cups flour
1 teaspoon vanilla

14. Martha decides to double the recipe. How much brown sugar will she use?

15. At the tea shop, $\frac{5}{15}$ of the customers purchased green tea, $\frac{2}{15}$ of the customers purchased jasmine tea, and $\frac{5}{15}$ of the customers purchased herbal tea. What portion of the customers purchased another type of tea?

16. A piece of fabric is $\frac{7}{9}$ yard long. A piece of ribbon is $\frac{2}{9}$ yard long. How many more yards of ribbon do you need to have equal lengths of fabric and ribbon?

Skill: Adding and Subtracting Mixed Numbers

Find each sum or difference.

1. $4\frac{3}{10} + 5\frac{2}{5}$

2. $3\frac{7}{8} + 2\frac{1}{2}$

3. $5\frac{2}{3} + 3\frac{1}{4}$

4. $6\frac{3}{4} + 2\frac{1}{2}$

5. $1\frac{1}{12} + 3\frac{1}{6}$

6. $9\frac{2}{5} + 10\frac{3}{10}$

7. $7\frac{1}{3} + 5\frac{11}{12}$

8. $11\frac{7}{10} + 4$

9. $2\frac{2}{3} + 4\frac{3}{4}$

10. $10\frac{11}{16} - 3\frac{7}{8}$

11. $8\frac{1}{3} - 2\frac{3}{8}$

12. $9 - 3\frac{2}{5}$

Skill: Adding and Subtracting Mixed Numbers (continued)

13. $5\frac{3}{16} - 2\frac{3}{8}$ **14.** $8\frac{1}{6} - 3\frac{2}{5}$ **15.** $7\frac{1}{2} - 3$

16. $2\frac{3}{4} - 1\frac{1}{8}$ **17.** $4\frac{1}{8} - 2\frac{1}{16}$ **18.** $9\frac{2}{3} - 3\frac{5}{6}$

19. Sam grew three pumpkins for the pumpkin growing contest. The pumpkins weighed $24\frac{1}{8}$ pounds, $18\frac{2}{4}$ pounds, and $32\frac{5}{16}$ pounds. Find the combined total weight of Sam's pumpkins.

20. Robbie needs to buy fencing for his square vegetable garden that measures $16\frac{3}{4}$ feet on a side. One side borders the back of the garage. The fencing costs $4 per feet. Estimate how much the fencing will cost.

Additional Practice

1. Phyllis is training for a marathon and wants to keep track of how far she runs each week. This week she ran $3\frac{1}{4}$ miles. She ran $\frac{2}{3}$ of them on Saturday. How many miles did Phyllis run on Saturday?

   a. Estimate the answer.

   b. Draw a model or diagram to find the exact answer.

   c. Write a number sentence for this situation.

Additional Practice (continued)

2. In a recent survey of 440 people, $\frac{1}{4}$ said that they watched television every evening, $\frac{2}{5}$ said they watched five or six nights each week, and the remainder said they watched four nights a week or less.

   a. How many people in the survey watched television every evening? Explain how you found your answer.

   b. How many people surveyed watched television five or six nights each week?

   c. What fraction of the people surveyed watched television four nights each week or less? Explain how you found your answer.

   d. How many people surveyed watch television four nights each week or less?

Additional Practice (continued)

3. Jack and Phil are selling advertisements for the yearbook. A full-page ad will cost $240. Advertisers who want only a fraction of a page will be charged that fraction of $240. Jack and Phil's layout for one page is shown at the right.

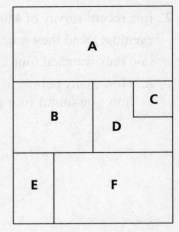

a. What fraction of the whole page does each of the six regions occupy?

b. How much should Jack and Phil charge an advertiser who wants to place an ad that fills area A? Explain how you found your answer.

c. How much should Jack and Phil charge an advertiser who wants to place an ad that fills area D?

d. How much should an ad that fills area F cost?

e. Jack and Phil have sold advertising space in areas B, E, and C.

   i. How much did they collect for the three ads?

   ii. What fraction of the page is left for other advertisers?

Additional Practice *(continued)*

4. A recipe for granola cookies calls for $\frac{1}{2}$ cup of butter and $\frac{1}{4}$ cup of chopped nuts. Because Jane likes moist cookies without too many nuts, she decides to increase the amount of butter by half and decrease the amount of chopped nuts by half.

a. How much butter is required for Jane's new recipe? Explain how you got your answer.

b. What amount of chopped nuts is required for Jane's new recipe? Explain your reasoning.

c. Since Jane increased the butter by half and decreased the nuts by half, is the combined amount of butter and nuts the same as in the original recipe? Explain why or why not.

5. Paul has $\frac{3}{5}$ of a roll of speaker wire left. His sister uses $\frac{1}{4}$ of it to set up speakers in her room.

a. How much of the whole roll of speaker wire did Paul's sister use?

b. What fraction of the whole roll is left? Explain your answer.

Additional Practice *(continued)*

6. For each set of multiplication problems, determine whether the products are equal or whether one product is greater. Describe any patterns you see.

a. $\frac{1}{3} \times \frac{2}{5}$ and $\frac{2}{3} \times \frac{1}{5}$

b. $\frac{7}{8} \times \frac{6}{5}$ and $\frac{6}{8} \times \frac{7}{5}$

c. $\frac{3}{10} \times \frac{5}{9}$ and $\frac{5}{10} \times \frac{3}{9}$

d. $\frac{3}{7} \times \frac{5}{8}$ and $\frac{5}{7} \times \frac{3}{8}$

7. If each person in North America throws away $3\frac{2}{3}$ pounds of garbage each day, how many pounds of garbage does each person throw away in a year?

Additional Practice: Digital Assessments

8. Which models can be used to find $\frac{1}{4} \times \frac{2}{3}$? *Select all that apply.*

☐

☐

☐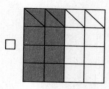

☐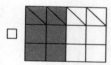

☐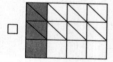

9. Circle the number that makes each statement true.

a. $\dfrac{4}{5} \times \dfrac{1}{3} = \begin{bmatrix} \dfrac{5}{8} \\ \dfrac{4}{15} \\ \dfrac{5}{15} \\ \dfrac{12}{5} \end{bmatrix}$

b. $1\dfrac{1}{4} \times 2\dfrac{1}{6} = \begin{bmatrix} 2\dfrac{5}{12} \\ 2\dfrac{17}{24} \\ 3\dfrac{1}{10} \end{bmatrix}$

c. $\dfrac{2}{3}$ of $5 = \begin{bmatrix} \dfrac{10}{15} \\ 2\dfrac{5}{3} \\ 3\dfrac{1}{3} \end{bmatrix}$

10. Write one of the symbols from the tiles on each line to create true statements.

$\dfrac{2}{5} \times \dfrac{1}{2} \; \boxed{\phantom{<}} \; \dfrac{1}{3} \times \dfrac{3}{5}$ $\dfrac{1}{3} \times \dfrac{1}{2} \; \boxed{\phantom{<}} \; \dfrac{1}{3} \times \dfrac{1}{3}$

$\dfrac{3}{7} \times \dfrac{4}{5} \; \boxed{\phantom{<}} \; \dfrac{4}{9} \times \dfrac{2}{5}$ $\dfrac{1}{5} \times \dfrac{2}{5} \; \boxed{\phantom{<}} \; \dfrac{3}{5} \times \dfrac{2}{5}$

Skill: Multiplying Fractions

Draw a model to find each product.

1. $\frac{1}{6} \times \frac{3}{4}$

2. $\frac{2}{5} \times \frac{1}{2}$

Find each product.

3. $\frac{3}{5}$ of 10

4. $\frac{1}{4}$ of 12

5. $\frac{2}{3}$ of 6

6. $\frac{4}{5}$ of $\frac{5}{8}$

7. $\frac{5}{6}$ of $\frac{3}{8}$

8. $\frac{3}{5}$ of $\frac{1}{2}$

9. $\frac{3}{4}$ of 12

10. $\frac{2}{5}$ of 15

Skill: Multiplying Fractions (continued)

11. $\frac{3}{5}$ of $\frac{3}{4}$

12. $\frac{1}{2} \times \frac{1}{3}$

13. $\frac{1}{8} \times \frac{3}{4}$

14. $\frac{2}{5} \times \frac{7}{11}$

15. $\frac{2}{3}$ of $\frac{1}{4}$

16. $\frac{2}{5} \times \frac{1}{2}$

17. $\frac{1}{4}$ of $\frac{4}{5}$

18. $\frac{5}{6} \times \frac{2}{5}$

19. A kitten eats $\frac{1}{4}$ cup of cat food. Another cat in the same household eats 6 times as much. How much food does the cat eat?

Skill: Multiplying Mixed Numbers

Find each product.

1. $2\frac{5}{6} \times 1\frac{3}{4}$

2. $3\frac{3}{8} \times 7\frac{1}{4}$

3. $5\frac{3}{8} \times 2\frac{7}{8}$

4. $\frac{1}{4} \times 5\frac{2}{5}$

5. $1\frac{1}{2} \times 5\frac{1}{3}$

6. $\frac{3}{4} \times 1\frac{3}{5}$

7. $3\frac{1}{3} \times 3\frac{3}{10}$

8. $5\frac{1}{2} \times \frac{2}{5}$

9. $1\frac{2}{3} \times 3\frac{3}{4}$

Skill: Multiplying Mixed Numbers (continued)

10. Ken used all of a piece of lumber to build a bookshelf. If he made three shelves that are each $2\frac{1}{2}$ feet long, how long was the piece of lumber?

11. Deanna's cake recipe needs to be doubled for a party. How much of each ingredient should Deanna use?

Cake Recipe		
Ingredient	Amount	Doubled amount
flour	$2\frac{1}{4}$ cups	
sugar	$1\frac{3}{4}$ cups	
butter	$1\frac{1}{2}$ cups	
milk	$\frac{3}{4}$ cup	

Additional Practice

1. Deb has 26 ounces of shredded cheese. She is making 4 small loaves of garlic cheese bread. Use the model below to help answer exercises (a)–(b).

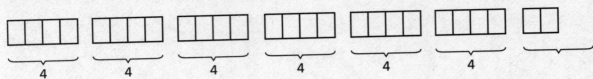

a. How many ounces of cheese can Deb use in each loaf of bread? Explain your reasoning.

b. Write a number sentence showing your calculations.

2. LiAnn works in the Olde Tyme Soda Shoppe. The shop sells milkshakes, double milkshakes, and triple milkshakes. A shake uses $\frac{1}{8}$ cup of syrup, a double shake uses $\frac{1}{4}$ cup of syrup, and a triple shake uses $\frac{3}{8}$ cup of syrup. How many shakes of each kind could she make with 3 cups of syrup?

Additional Practice *(continued)*

3. Three groups of students are sharing leftover pizza (all the same size originally). In which group does each student get the most pizza? Explain your choice.

   Group 1: Six students equally share $\frac{3}{4}$ of a pizza.

   Group 2: Three students equally share $\frac{1}{3}$ of a pizza.

   Group 3: Four students equally share $\frac{2}{3}$ of a pizza.

4. Find each quotient.

   a. $12 \div \frac{1}{2}$

   b. $12 \div \frac{1}{3}$

   c. $3 \div \frac{2}{3}$

   d. $\frac{7}{8} \div 4$

   e. $1\frac{2}{3} \div 6$

   f. $\frac{5}{6} \div \frac{1}{3}$

   g. $1\frac{1}{4} \div 2\frac{1}{2}$

   h. $\frac{8}{5} \div \frac{3}{10}$

   i. $1\frac{1}{2} \div \frac{3}{4}$

Additional Practice (continued)

5. Max noticed a pattern in some fraction division problems that he computed.

$$\frac{6}{8} \div \frac{3}{8} \text{ gives the same answer as } 6 \div 3.$$

$$\frac{7}{10} \div \frac{3}{10} \text{ gives the same answer as } 7 \div 3.$$

$$\frac{9}{5} \div \frac{2}{5} \text{ gives the same answer as } 9 \div 2.$$

$$\frac{4}{7} \div \frac{5}{7} \text{ gives the same answer as } 4 \div 5.$$

Describe the pattern that Max found. Explain why it works.

6. Sam, Trish, and Shanti are making signs for the spring dance. Sam can make a sign in $\frac{3}{4}$ of an hour, Trish can make a sign in $\frac{2}{3}$ of an hour, and Shanti can make a sign in $\frac{3}{5}$ of an hour.

   a. How many complete signs can each person make in 4 hours?

   b. Who has the most time left over after finishing his or her last complete sign? How do you know?

7. How many bows can you make from 5 meters of ribbon if making a bow takes $\frac{1}{4}$ of a meter of ribbon?

Additional Practice: Digital Assessments

Let's Be Rational

8. Circle the number that makes each statement true.

a. $\dfrac{2}{5} \div \dfrac{2}{3} = \begin{bmatrix} \dfrac{5}{3} \\ \dfrac{3}{5} \\ \dfrac{4}{15} \end{bmatrix}$

b. $4\dfrac{2}{7} \div 2 = \begin{bmatrix} 2\dfrac{1}{7} \\ 2\dfrac{2}{7} \\ 8\dfrac{4}{7} \end{bmatrix}$

c. $3\dfrac{4}{5} \div 2\dfrac{1}{5} = \begin{bmatrix} 1\dfrac{3}{5} \\ 1\dfrac{8}{11} \\ 6\dfrac{4}{25} \end{bmatrix}$

9. Each step that Brooke takes is $\dfrac{2}{3}$ of a meter. Which expressions can be used to find how many steps she will take if she walks 50 meters? *Select all that apply.*

☐ $\dfrac{2}{3} \div 50$

☐ $50 \div \dfrac{2}{3}$

☐ $\dfrac{2}{3} \times 50$

☐ $50 \times \dfrac{2}{3}$

10. Write each expression in the box with the correct category.

$$\dfrac{5}{9} \div \dfrac{2}{9} \qquad \dfrac{9}{5} \div \dfrac{9}{2} \qquad \dfrac{10}{7} \div \dfrac{4}{7} \qquad \dfrac{5}{6} \div \dfrac{1}{3} \qquad \dfrac{3}{4} \div \dfrac{15}{8}$$

$\dfrac{5}{2}$	$\dfrac{2}{5}$

Skill: Dividing Fractions

1. Draw a diagram to show how many $\frac{3}{4}$-foot pieces of string can be cut from a piece of string $4\frac{1}{2}$ feet long.

Find each quotient.

2. $\frac{1}{12} \div \frac{5}{6}$

3. $4 \div \frac{1}{3}$

4. $6 \div \frac{3}{4}$

5. $5 \div \frac{9}{10}$

6. $8 \div \frac{2}{3}$

7. $\frac{4}{5} \div 2$

8. $\frac{7}{8} \div 3$

9. $\frac{5}{6} \div 5$

10. $\frac{4}{9} \div 8$

11. $\frac{3}{4} \div \frac{1}{4}$

12. $\frac{7}{8} \div \frac{1}{4}$

13. $\frac{5}{6} \div \frac{1}{12}$

14. How many $\frac{3}{4}$-cup servings are there in a 6-cup package of rice?

15. Study the tangram pieces at the right. If the entire square is 1, find the fractional value of each piece. You can copy the tangram and cut the pieces to compare them.

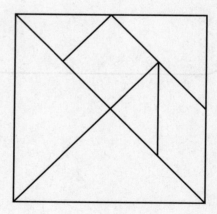

Skill: Dividing Mixed Numbers

Find each quotient.

1. $1\frac{1}{2} \div \frac{2}{3}$

2. $1\frac{1}{2} \div \frac{3}{2}$

3. $\frac{3}{4} \div 1\frac{1}{3}$

4. $2\frac{1}{2} \div 1\frac{1}{4}$

5. $2\frac{1}{2} \div 2\frac{1}{4}$

6. $1\frac{3}{4} \div \frac{3}{4}$

7. $1\frac{7}{10} \div \frac{1}{2}$

8. $3\frac{1}{4} \div 1\frac{1}{3}$

9. $4\frac{1}{2} \div 2\frac{1}{2}$

10. $6 \div 3\frac{4}{5}$

11. $4\frac{3}{4} \div \frac{7}{8}$

12. $5\frac{5}{6} \div 1\frac{1}{3}$

13. Rosa makes $2\frac{1}{2}$ cups of pudding. How many $\frac{1}{3}$-cup servings can she get from the pudding?

14. One type of lightning bug glows once every $1\frac{1}{2}$ seconds. How many times can it glow in 1 minute?

15. Bea can run $\frac{1}{6}$ mile in 2 minutes. How long should it take her to run 2 miles?

Additional Practice

1. For each number sentence, write a complete fact family.

a. $\frac{3}{7} + \frac{1}{3} = \frac{16}{21}$

b. $\frac{11}{12} - \frac{3}{8} = \frac{13}{24}$

c. $\frac{1}{6} + N = \frac{11}{12}$

d. $\frac{13}{15} - N = \frac{1}{6}$

e. $N + 1\frac{1}{4} = 3\frac{5}{8}$

f. $N - \frac{5}{2} = \frac{7}{6}$

Additional Practice (continued)

2. For each number sentence, find the value of N.

a. $N + \frac{2}{5} = \frac{7}{10}$

b. $N - \frac{1}{3} = \frac{3}{11}$

c. $\frac{3}{4} + N = \frac{8}{5}$

d. $\frac{17}{12} - N = \frac{2}{3}$

e. $1\frac{3}{8} + N = 2\frac{1}{4}$

f. $4\frac{4}{9} - N = 3\frac{1}{3}$

g. $1\frac{1}{2} + N + \frac{3}{4} = 3\frac{1}{3}$

h. $N - \frac{5}{6} = \frac{8}{15} - \frac{1}{9}$

Additional Practice (continued)

3. For each number sentence, write a complete fact family.

   a. $\frac{2}{5} \times \frac{3}{4} = \frac{3}{10}$ **b.** $\frac{8}{9} \div \frac{2}{3} = \frac{4}{3}$

   c. $N \times \frac{1}{2} = \frac{4}{5}$ **d.** $N \div \frac{3}{5} = \frac{2}{3}$

   e. $\frac{2}{3} \times N = 1\frac{1}{6}$ **f.** $1\frac{1}{12} \div N = \frac{13}{8}$

Additional Practice (continued)

4. Find the value of N that makes each number sentence true.

a. $N \times \frac{5}{6} = \frac{10}{3}$

b. $N \div \frac{2}{7} = \frac{3}{2}$

c. $\frac{5}{8} \times N = \frac{5}{4}$

d. $\frac{35}{12} \div N = \frac{5}{3}$

e. $N \times \frac{4}{5} = 2\frac{4}{5}$

f. $2\frac{1}{24} \div N = 1\frac{1}{6}$

g. $N \times \frac{1}{3} \times \frac{2}{3} = \frac{4}{9}$

h. $\frac{3}{5} \times \frac{1}{2} = \frac{9}{10} \div N$

Additional Practice (continued)

5. A hare can travel $\frac{3}{4}$ mile in one minute. The fastest recorded speed of a tortoise is $\frac{1}{12}$ mile per minute.

   a. How much farther can a hare travel in one minute than a tortoise?

   b. How far will the hare travel in $4\frac{1}{2}$ minutes?

   c. How long will it take the tortoise to travel $\frac{4}{5}$ mile?

6. A recipe for the dressing of a large fruit salad calls for $\frac{1}{2}$ cup apple cider vinegar, $\frac{1}{3}$ cup lemon juice, and $\frac{1}{4}$ cup honey.

   a. How much dressing is made from 1 batch of the recipe?

   b. There is $\frac{5}{8}$ cup of honey left in the jar. How much apple cider vinegar and lemon juice should be added to create some of the fruit salad dressing?

Additional Practice (continued)

7. Jill has a photograph that is a $3\frac{1}{2}$-inch square. She wants to attach it to a square piece of paper that is $8\frac{1}{2}$ inches on each side.

    a. How far from each edge should Jill align the edges of the photograph to center it exactly?

    b. What is the area of paper not covered by the photograph?

Additional Practice: Digital Assessments

8. Circle the correct solution for N.

a. $\frac{4}{3} - N = \frac{11}{12}$ 　　 $N = \begin{bmatrix} \dfrac{1}{3} \\ \dfrac{16}{11} \\ \dfrac{5}{12} \\ \dfrac{27}{12} \end{bmatrix}$

b. $N \times \frac{8}{15} = \frac{2}{3}$ 　　 $N = \begin{bmatrix} \dfrac{4}{5} \\ \dfrac{5}{4} \\ \dfrac{18}{15} \\ \dfrac{45}{16} \end{bmatrix}$

9. Choose the expressions that belong to the fact family of $\frac{2}{3} - \frac{1}{5} = \frac{7}{15}$. *Select all that apply.*

☐ $\frac{2}{3} - \frac{7}{15} = \frac{1}{5}$

☐ $\frac{2}{3} + \frac{1}{5} = \frac{7}{15}$

☐ $\frac{2}{3} = \frac{7}{15} - \frac{1}{5}$

☐ $\frac{2}{3} = \frac{1}{5} + \frac{7}{15}$

☐ $\frac{2}{3} = \frac{7}{15} + \frac{1}{5}$

10. Chase's soccer ball is $\frac{5}{8}$ full with air. Chase wants to know how much more of the ball must be filled with air for the ball to be $\frac{3}{4}$ filled with air. Using only the numbers and symbols on the tiles provided below, fill in each space to write an equation that can be used to model this situation.

| N | $\dfrac{5}{8}$ | $\dfrac{3}{4}$ | $+$ | $-$ | $\times$ | $\div$ |

☐ ☐ ☐ $=$ ☐

Skill: Writing Number Sentences

Write a number sentence to represent the situation. Then solve.

1. Half of a number is $\frac{4}{7}$. What is the number?

2. The pitcher had $1\frac{1}{4}$ quarts of water. After Lena poured some of the water into a bowl, the pitcher had $\frac{1}{2}$ quart of water left. How much water was poured in the bowl?

3. Each bag of trail mix weighs $\frac{3}{8}$ pound. The combined weight of a set of bags is $3\frac{3}{4}$ pounds. How many bags are there?

4. Ben needs to run $4\frac{1}{2}$ miles. He has already run $1\frac{2}{3}$ miles. How many miles does he have left to run?

Skill: Writing Number Sentences (continued)

5. Water flows through the pipe at a rate of $\frac{2}{5}$ gallon per minute. How much water has traveled through the pipe after 10 minutes?

6. The cat weighs $7\frac{3}{4}$ pounds. The cat's weight is $\frac{2}{3}$ the weight of the dog. How much does the dog weigh?

7. The recipe calls for $3\frac{1}{3}$ cups of flour. The bag has $2\frac{1}{4}$ cups of flour. How much more flour is needed?

8. A large piece of fabric measures 20 square yards. It is divided into sections that are $1\frac{1}{2}$ square yards each. How many whole sections are there?

Additional Practice

1. Find the area and the perimeter of each of the four shapes below.

a.

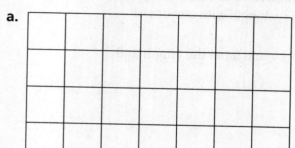

b.

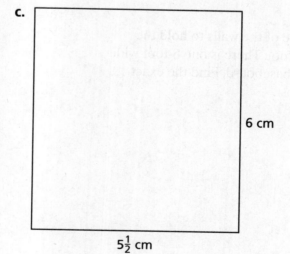

c.

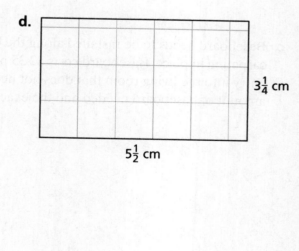

6 cm

$5\frac{1}{2}$ cm

d.

$3\frac{1}{4}$ cm

$5\frac{1}{2}$ cm

Additional Practice (continued)

2. Susan is helping her father measure the living room floor because they want to buy new carpeting. The floor is in the shape of a rectangle with a width of 10 feet and a length of 14 feet.

   a. Draw a sketch that shows the shape of the floor and label the length and width.

   b. If the carpeting costs $1.75 per square foot, how much will it cost to buy the exact amount of carpeting needed to carpet the living room?

   c. Baseboard needs to be installed along the base of the walls to hold the carpeting in place. Baseboard costs $2.35 per foot. There is one 6-foot wide entry into the living room that does not need baseboard. Find the exact amount of baseboard needed and the exact cost.

Additional Practice (continued)

3. Ellen drew a rectangle. She says the area of her rectangle is 7 square units and the perimeter is 16 units. Could Ellen be correct about the perimeter and area of her rectangle? Explain.

4. Use the diagram below to answer the following questions. (All angles in the diagram are right angles.)

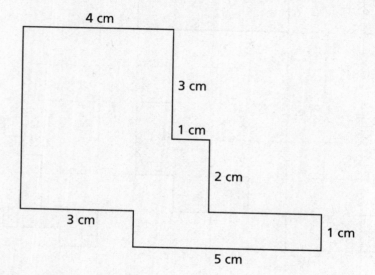

4 cm

3 cm

1 cm

2 cm

3 cm

1 cm

5 cm

a. What is the perimeter of the figure?

b. What is the area of the figure?

c. Explain how you found your answers for parts (a) and (b).

Additional Practice *(continued)*

5. Find the area and perimeter of each figure below.

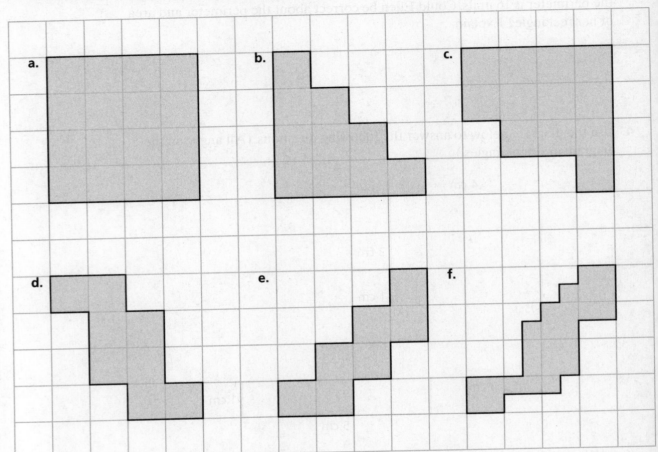

6. Find the area and perimeter of each of the following rectangles.

Rectangle	Area	Perimeter
a. 3 in. ☐ 7 in.		
b. ☐ $3\frac{1}{2}$ in. $3\frac{1}{2}$ in.		
c. Length: 25 cm; width: 8 cm		
d. Length: $6\frac{3}{4}$ cm; width: $4\frac{7}{8}$ cm		

Additional Practice (continued)

7. a. Give the dimensions of the rectangle with an area of 100 square units and whole-number side lengths that has

    i. the largest perimeter

    ii. the smallest perimeter

  b. Explain how you found your answers in part (a).

8. Jim has designed a rectangular garden with an area of 20 square yards and a perimeter of 81 yards.

  a. Find the dimensions of all of the possible rectangles with whole-number side lengths that have an area of 20 units. Record the length, width, area, and perimeter in a table.

  b. Is it possible that Jim's garden has whole-number of yards as side lengths? Explain.

  c. Jim used fractional dimensions to make his garden. What are its dimensions?

Additional Practice (continued)

9. Claire and Chad want to design a rectangular pen for their new puppy. They want the pen to have an area of 48 square feet. Fencing costs $0.85 per foot.

   a. What are the dimensions and the cost of the least expensive pen Claire and Chad could build, assuming the side lengths are whole numbers? Explain.

   b. What are the dimensions and the cost of the most expensive pen Claire and Chad could build, assuming the side lengths are whole numbers? Explain.

   c. Give the dimensions and the cost of a rectangular pen with whole-number side lengths and a cost between the least and most expensive pens you found in parts (a) and (b).

   d. Of the three pens you found, which one would you suggest that Claire and Chad build? Explain your choice.

Additional Practice *(continued)*

10. Is each perimeter possible for a rectangle with an area of 42 square units and whole-number side lengths? If so, give the dimensions.

   a. 28 units   **b.** 46 units   **c.** 34 units   **d.** 41 units

11. Find the dimensions of all the possible rectangles with whole-number side lengths that have a perimeter of 10 units. Record the length, width, area, and perimeter in a table. Explain how you made sure you did not miss any rectangles.

12. Is each area possible for a rectangle with a perimeter of 28 units and whole-number side lengths? If so, give the dimensions.

   a. 24 sq. units   **b.** 40 sq. units   **c.** 42 sq. units   **d.** 45 sq. units

Additional Practice *(continued)*

13. Tracy has 40 feet of material to make the perimeter of a rectangular sandbox for her little brother.

    a. What rectangle with whole-number side lengths would give the sandbox with the greatest area?

    b. What rectangle with whole-number side lengths would give the sandbox with the least area?

    c. Give the dimensions of a rectangle with whole-number side lengths that has an area between the least and greatest areas you found in parts (a) and (b).

    d. Of the three rectangles you found, which one would you recommend that Tracy make? Explain your reasoning.

Additional Practice (continued)

14. Travis designs a rectangle with an area of 59 square units. The side lengths are whole numbers.

   a. What are the length and width of the rectangle? Explain your reasoning.

   b. What is the perimeter of the rectangle?

   c. What is the area of the largest rectangle that Travis could make with the same perimeter?

15. Helen designs a rectangle with an area of 225 square units. Her rectangle is the largest rectangle (that is, the rectangle with largest area) with whole-number side lengths that can be made from the perimeter of the rectangle.

   a. What are the length and width of the rectangle?

   b. What is the perimeter of the rectangle?

Additional Practice: Digital Assessments

Covering and Surrounding

16. Shade part of the grid to form a figure that has an area of 33 square units.

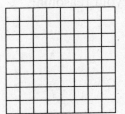

17. Shade part of the grid to form a figure that has a perimeter of 24 units.

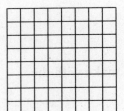

18. You want to plant a rectangular garden with an area of 64 square feet.

  a. What are the possible dimensions of the garden? *Select all that apply.*

    ☐ 1 foot × 64 feet

    ☐ 2 feet × 48 feet

    ☐ 2 feet × 32 feet

    ☐ 4 feet × 16 feet

    ☐ 6 feet × 12 feet

    ☐ 8 feet × 8 feet

  b. A fence will be built around the garden. Circle the dimensions for the garden that will require the least amount of fencing to enclose.

$$\begin{bmatrix} 1 \\ 2 \\ 4 \\ 6 \\ 8 \end{bmatrix} \text{feet} \times \begin{bmatrix} 8 \\ 12 \\ 16 \\ 32 \\ 48 \\ 64 \end{bmatrix} \text{feet}$$

19. Four rectangles have the dimensions given on the tiles.

    (1 cm × 11 cm) (4 cm × 7 cm) (3 cm × 5 cm) (2 cm × 7 cm)

  a. Order the dimensions of the rectangles from shortest perimeter to longest perimeter.

    ☐ , ☐ , ☐ , ☐

  b. Order the dimensions of the rectangles from smallest area to largest area.

    ☐ , ☐ , ☐ , ☐

Skill: Area and Perimeter of Rectangles

Find the perimeter and area of each rectangle.

1.

8 cm

15 cm

2.

12 in.

20 in.

3.

6 cm

6 cm

4. $\ell = 5$ in., $w = 13$ in.

5. $\ell = 18$ m, $w = 12$ m

6. $\ell = 3$ ft, $w = 8$ ft

7. rectangle: $l = 16$ mm, $w = 12$ mm

8. rectangle: $l = 65$ mi, $w = 48$ mi

9. The length of a rectangle is 8 centimeters. The width is 6 centimeters.

   a. What is the area?

   b. What is the perimeter?

10. The area of a rectangle is 45 square inches. One dimension is 5 inches. What is the perimeter?

Skill: Area and Perimeter of Rectangles *(continued)*

Find the area of each rectangle or composition of rectangles.

11.
4 m
4 m

12.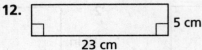
5 cm
23 cm

13.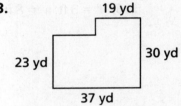
19 yd
30 yd
23 yd
37 yd

14.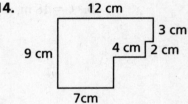
12 cm
3 cm
4 cm 2 cm
9 cm
7cm

15. The figure at the right contains only squares.
Each side of the shaded square is 1 unit.
What is the length, width, and area of the figure?

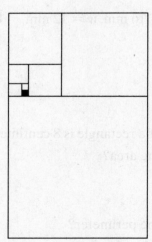

16. The perimeter of a rectangle is 38 centimeters.
The length is $7\frac{1}{2}$ centimeters. What is the width?

Skill: Changing Area, Changing Perimeter

Covering and Surrounding

Solve.

1. The perimeter of a rectangle is 72 meters. The width of the rectangle is 16 meters. What is the area of the rectangle?

2. You have 36 feet of fencing. What are the areas of the different rectangles you could enclose with the fencing? Consider only whole-number dimensions.

3. Corinda has 400 feet of fencing to make a play area. She wants the fenced area to be rectangular. What dimensions should she use in order to enclose the maximum possible area?

Additional Practice

1. Find the area and perimeter of each shape below.

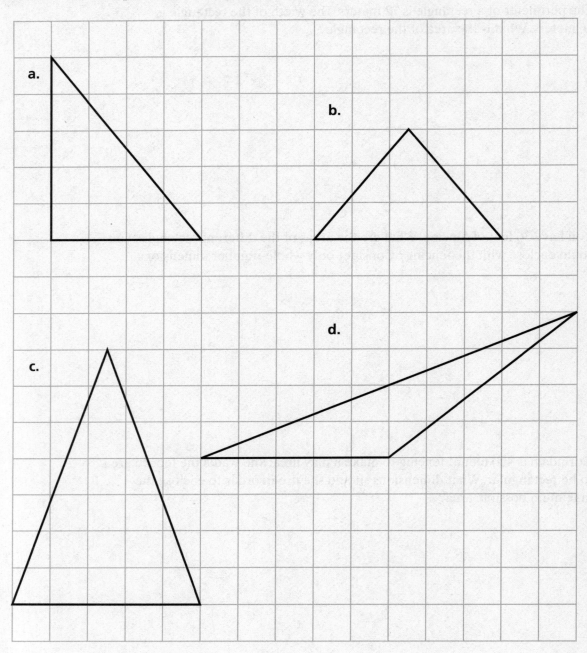

a.

b.

c.

d.

Additional Practice (continued)

2. a. Find the area of each triangle below.

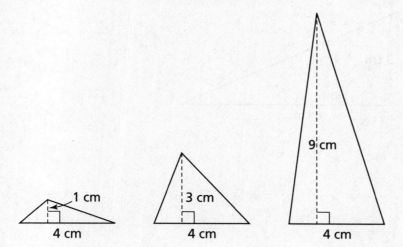

b. How are the heights of these triangles related to each other?

c. How are the areas of these triangles related to each other?

3. a. Find the area of each triangle below.

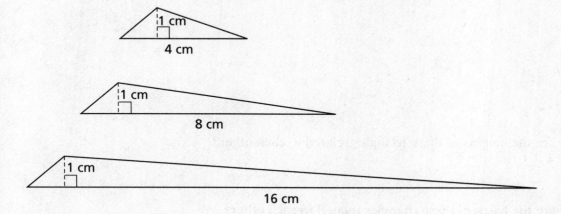

b. How are the bases of these triangles related to each other?

c. How are the areas of these triangles related to each other?

Additional Practice *(continued)*

4. a. Find the area of each triangle below.

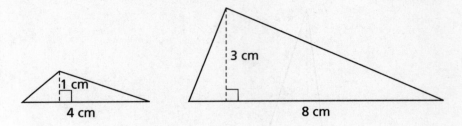

b. Based on the patterns in Exercises 2 and 3, sketch the third triangle.

c. How are the heights of these triangles related to each other?

d. How are the bases of these triangles related to each other?

e. How are the areas of these triangles related to each other?

Additional Practice: Digital Assessments

5. Select the triangles that have an area of 12 square inches. *Select all that apply*.

☐ A right triangle with a base of 6 inches and a height of 4 inches.

☐ A triangle with a base of 4 inches and a height of 3 inches.

☐ A triangle with a base of 12 inches and a height of 1 inch.

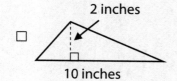

2 inches

☐

10 inches

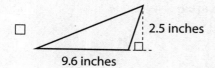

☐

2.5 inches

9.6 inches

6. Circle the number that makes each statement true.

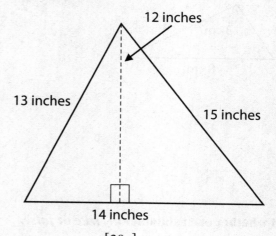

12 inches

13 inches

15 inches

14 inches

a. The area is $\begin{bmatrix} 30 \\ 42 \\ 84 \\ 105 \\ 168 \end{bmatrix}$ square inches.

b. The perimeter is $\begin{bmatrix} 39 \\ 42 \\ 54 \\ 58 \\ 84 \end{bmatrix}$ inches.

7. The area of the triangle is 56 square meters and the perimeter is 44 meters. Use the values in the box to fill in the lengths of the sides of the triangle and its height.

| 7 meters | 11 meters | 14 meters |
| 8 meters | 12 meters | 18 meters |

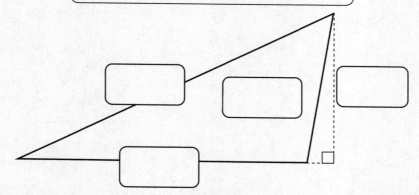

Skill: Area of Triangles

Find the area of each triangle.

4.

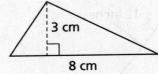

3 cm
8 cm

2.

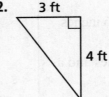

3 ft
4 ft

Tell whether each statement is *true* or *false*.

3. Two triangles that have the same base always have the same area.

4. Any obtuse triangle has a greater area than any acute triangle.

Find the area and perimeter of each triangle.

5.

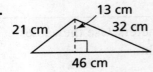

13 cm
21 cm   32 cm
46 cm

6.

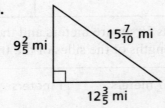

$15\frac{7}{10}$ mi
$9\frac{2}{5}$ mi
$12\frac{3}{5}$ mi

Skill: Area of Triangles (continued)

Covering and Surrounding

Find the area of each triangle.

7.

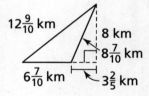

$12\frac{9}{10}$ km   8 km $8\frac{7}{10}$ km $6\frac{7}{10}$ km $3\frac{2}{5}$ km

8.

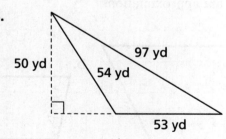

50 yd   97 yd   54 yd   53 yd

Solve.

9. The area of a triangle is 6 square units. Both the height and the length of the base are whole numbers. What are the possible lengths and heights?

Name _____ Date _____ Class _____

Additional Practice

1. For each of the following, find the perimeter and area of the parallelogram. Labeled lengths are approximations.

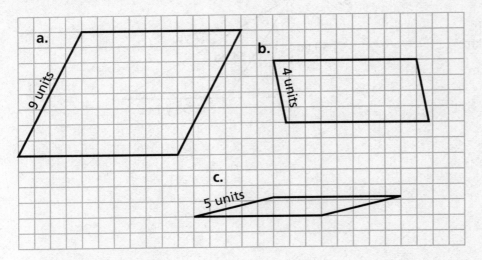

2. Use the diagram below to answer the following questions.

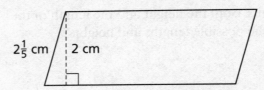

a. If the perimeter of the parallelogram is $14\frac{2}{5}$ centimeters, what is the length of the base?

b. What is the area of the parallelogram?

Additional Practice (continued)

3. The area of a parallelogram is 24 square centimeters, and the base of the parallelogram is 6 centimeters.

   a. What is the height of the parallelogram?

   b. If the perimeter of the parallelogram is 22 centimeters, what is the length of the other side of the parallelogram (that is, the side that isn't the base)?

4. **a.** Find the area of each parallelogram below.

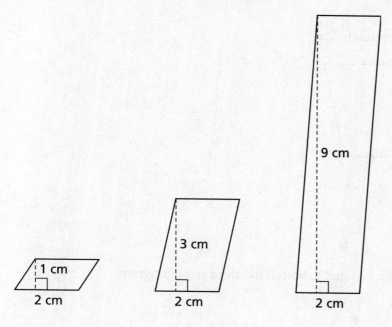

   b. How are the heights of these parallelograms related to each other?

   c. How are the areas of these parallelograms related to each other?

Additional Practice (continued)

5. **a.** Find the area of each parallelogram below.

 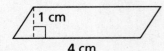 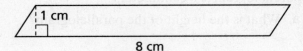

b. How are the bases of these parallelograms related to each other?

c. How are the areas of these parallelograms related to each other?

6. **a.** Find the area of each parallelogram below.

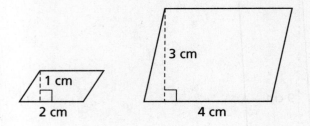

b. Based on the patterns in Exercises 4 and 5, sketch the third parallelogram beside the first two.

c. How are the heights of these parallelograms related to each other?

d. How are the bases of these parallelograms related to each other?

e. How are the areas of these parallelograms related to each other?

Additional Practice (continued)

7. The parallelogram shown below is missing coordinates for one of its vertices.

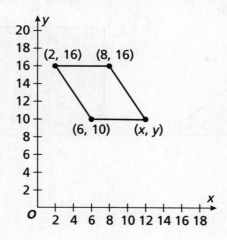

a. Find the missing coordinates.

b. Find the area of the parallelogram.

8. a. Find the area and perimeter of the right triangle below.

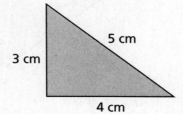

Additional Practice (continued)

b. Each figure below is made from copies of the triangle from part (a). Find the area and perimeter of each figure.

i.

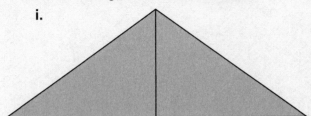

ii.

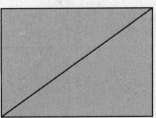

iii.

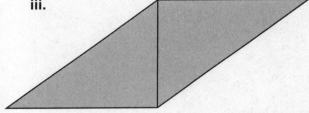

iv.

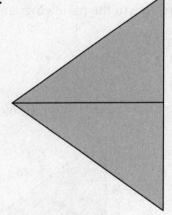

Additional Practice: Digital Assessments

9. The coordinates of two vertices of a parallelogram are $(3, 2)$ and $(7, 2)$. The parallelogram has an area of 12 square units. Which of the following could be the coordinates of the third and fourth vertices? *Select all that apply.*

☐ $(1, 5)$ and $(4, 5)$

☐ $(2, 5)$ and $(6, 5)$

☐ $(3, 6)$ and $(7, 6)$

☐ $(5, 5)$ and $(9, 5)$

☐ $(0, 6)$ and $(4, 6)$

10. Circle the number that makes each statement true.

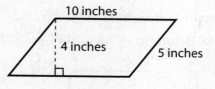

a. The area is $\begin{bmatrix} 20 \\ 25 \\ 30 \\ 40 \\ 45 \\ 50 \end{bmatrix}$ square inches.

b. The perimeter is $\begin{bmatrix} 15 \\ 19 \\ 30 \\ 38 \\ 40 \\ 50 \end{bmatrix}$ inches.

11. Write the correct set of measurements in each box.

Area = 35 square feet
Perimeter = 30 feet

Area = 36 square feet
Perimeter = 34 feet

Area = 60 square feet
Perimeter = 34 feet

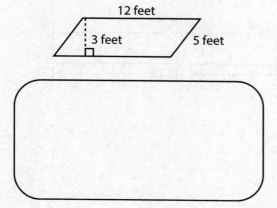

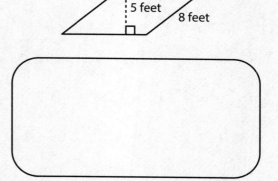

Additional Practice

1. The four nets below will fold into rectangular boxes. Net *iii* folds into an open box. The other nets fold into closed boxes. Answer the following questions for each net.

   a. What are the dimensions of the box that can be made from the net?

   b. What is the surface area of the box?

   c. What total number of unit cubes would be needed to fill the box?

   i.

   40 cm

   10 cm

   10 cm

   40 cm

   ii.

   5 cm

   5 cm

   5 cm

   5 cm

   iii.

   $2\frac{1}{2}$ cm

   $2\frac{1}{2}$ cm

   $2\frac{1}{2}$ cm

   iv.

   12 cm

   12 cm

   6 cm

   42 cm

Additional Practice (continued)

2. a. Gina has a sheet of cardboard that measures 9 feet by 6 feet. She uses scissors and tape to make the entire sheet of cardboard into a closed box that is a perfect cube. What is the surface area of the box?

b. What is the length of each edge of the box? Explain your reasoning.

c. How many unit cubes would it take to fill the box?

3. a. Bill has a sheet of cardboard with an area of 10 square feet. He makes the entire sheet of cardboard into a closed rectangular box. The four sides of the box have the same area, and the two ends have the same area. The area of each of the four equal sides is twice the area of each end. What is the area of each face of Bill's box?

b. What are the dimensions of Bill's box?

c. How many unit cubes would it take to fill the box?

Additional Practice (continued)

4. The bottom of a closed rectangular box has an area of 50 square centimeters. If the box is 8 centimeters high, give at least three possibilities for the dimensions of the box.

5. The rectangular prism below is made from centimeter cubes.

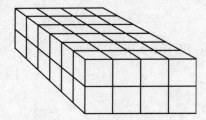

   a. What are the dimensions of the prism?

   b. What is the surface area of the prism?

   c. What is the volume of the prism? That is, how many cubes are in the prism?

   d. Give the dimensions of a different rectangular prism that can be made from the same number of cubes. What is the surface area of the prism?

Additional Practice *(continued)*

6. Use the diagram at the right to answer the following questions.

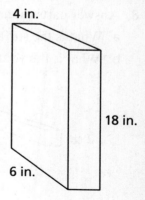

4 in.

18 in.

6 in.

a. What is the total surface area of the box, including the bottom and the top?

b. How many inch cubes would it take to fill the box? Explain your reasoning.

7. a. Each small cube in the rectangular prism at the right has edges of length 2 centimeters. What are the dimensions of the prism in centimeters?

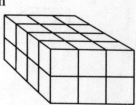

b. What is the surface area of the prism in square centimeters?

c. How many 1-centimeter cubes would it take to make a prism with the same dimensions as this prism? Explain your reasoning.

Additional Practice (continued)

8. Answer parts (a) and (b) for each closed box below.

   a. What is the surface area of each box?

   b. What is the volume of each box?

   i.

   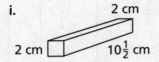

   ii.

   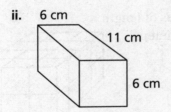

   iii.

   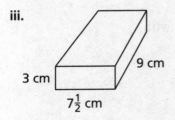

Additional Practice: Digital Assessments

9. Shade each grid to create different nets of a cube.

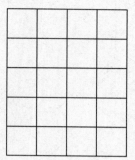

10. The height of a box is 3 feet. The volume of the box is 48 cubic feet. Which of the following could be the length and width?

Select all that apply.

☐ 4 ft × 6 ft

☐ 2.5 ft × 6.4 ft

☐ 3.2 ft × 5 ft

☐ 2 ft × 8 ft

☐ 2.5 ft × 4 ft

11. Circle the numbers that make each statement true.

a. The volume of a rectangular prism is 60 cm³.

The dimensions could be $\begin{bmatrix} 1\frac{1}{2} \\ 2 \\ 2\frac{1}{2} \\ 3 \\ 3\frac{1}{2} \end{bmatrix}$ cm by $\begin{bmatrix} 2 \\ 3 \\ 4 \\ 5 \\ 6 \end{bmatrix}$ cm by $7\frac{1}{2}$ cm.

b. The surface area of a rectangular prism is 62 cm².

The dimensions could be 2 cm by $\begin{bmatrix} 1 \\ 2 \\ 3 \\ 4 \\ 5 \end{bmatrix}$ cm by 5 cm.

Skill: Surface Area of a Box

Covering and Surrounding

Draw a net for each prism.

1.

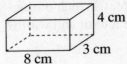

4 cm
8 cm
3 cm

2.

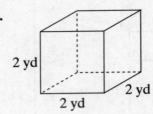

2 yd
2 yd
2 yd

Find the surface area of each figure.

3.

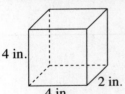

4 in.
4 in.
2 in.

4.

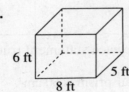

6 ft
8 ft
5 ft

5.

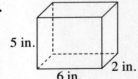

5 in.
6 in.
2 in.

6.

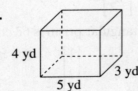

4 yd
5 yd
3 yd

Skill: Surface Area of a Box (continued)

Find the surface area of each prism.

7.

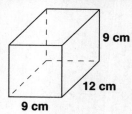

9 cm

12 cm

9 cm

8.

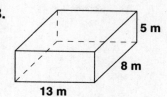

5 m

8 m

13 m

9.

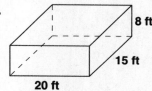

8 ft

15 ft

20 ft

10.

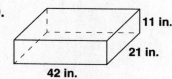

11 in.

21 in.

42 in.

11.

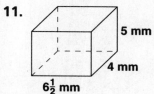

5 mm

4 mm

$6\frac{1}{2}$ mm

12.

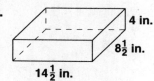

4 in.

$8\frac{1}{2}$ in.

$14\frac{1}{2}$ in.

Skill: Volume of a Box

Covering and Surrounding

Find the volume of each closed box.

1.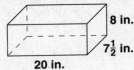

20 in. 8 in. $7\frac{1}{2}$ in.

2.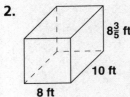

$8\frac{3}{5}$ ft 10 ft 8 ft

3.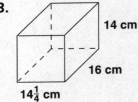

14 cm 16 cm $14\frac{1}{4}$ cm

Skill: Volume of a Box (continued)

Find the volume of each closed box.

4.

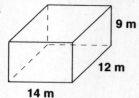

9 m

12 m

14 m

5.

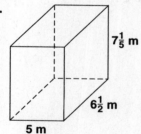

$7\frac{1}{5}$ m

$6\frac{1}{2}$ m

5 m

Name _____ Date _____ Class _____

Additional Practice

For Exercises 1–6,
   a. Write a number sentence for the problem.
   b. Estimate the answer.
   c. Use mental arithmetic, a calculator, or some other method to find the exact answer.
   d. Explain how your estimate helps you check the exact answer.

1. Ashley builds a rectangular dog pen. The width is 5.75 feet and the length is 7.25 feet. What is the area of the dog pen?

2. Tim is mailing some cards. Five cards each require $0.46 worth of postage. Two larger cards each require $0.92 worth of postage. What is the total postage Tim needs to pay?

3. Lamar has 3.6 meters of string. He makes a square with congruent sides. What is the length of each side?

Additional Practice (continued)

4. A grocer purchases 20.2 pounds of roast beef for a bulk rate price of $39.20. How much does the grocer pay per pound?

5. The grocer from Exercise 4 sells roast beef for $3.09 per pound. Ms. Smith has a coupon for $0.75 off her total. She purchases 1.52 pounds of roast beef. How much is her bill after the coupon?

6. A hiking guide recommends using a backpack that weighs no more than 25 pounds. Karin and Sarah each plan on taking a backpack on their hike. The table shows the weights of the items that they want to take.

1 liter of water: 2.2 pounds	Trail mix: 0.75 pound	Rain jacket: 1.1 pounds
Dry socks: 0.14 pound	Fresh fruit: 0.6 pound	Backpack: 1.7 pounds

Karin and Sarah each plan on packing 3 liters of water and one of each other item in her backpack for a 1-day hike. What is the total weight of one backpack?

Additional Practice (continued)

7. Ava has $20 gift card to spend at an online store. The table shows the prices of the digital downloads that are available.

Downloads	Cost
Single Song	$0.89
Music Album	$10.49
Game	$2.89
Ring-tone	$0.49

a. How many games could Ava purchase with the gift card?

b. Ava decides to buy 1 music album and spend the rest on games. How many games could Ava buy? How much money would be left on the gift card?

c. The music album Ava decides to buy has 12 songs. Is it cheaper to buy the music album or the 12 songs as singles? What is the difference in cost?

130

Additional Practice (continued)

8. The table shows the prices for four types of granola.

Type	Weight	Cost
Triple Berry	16 oz	$5.99
Chocolate Cherry	24 oz	$8.25
Honey Pecan	12 oz	$4.49
Seeds and Oats	10 oz	$3.99

a. Which granola is the least expensive per ounce? Most expensive per ounce? Explain.

b. How much would 32 ounces of each granola cost?

c. How much of each granola could be purchased with $10.00? Round to the nearest ounce.

d. Jamie mixes 16 ounces of Triple Berry granola with 10 ounces of Seed and Oats. What is the unit rate of mixture?

Additional Practice (continued)

9. The table shows the distances and winning times of a sprint triathlon.

Event	Distance	Winner	2nd place	3rd place
Swim	0.750 kilometer	10.3 minutes	10.2 minutes	11.1 minutes
Bike	20 kilometer	33.2 minutes	34.2 minutes	34.0 minutes
Run	5 kilometer	19.1 minutes	19.5 minutes	20.1 minutes

a. What was the winner's total time?

b. By how many minutes did the winner finish before the person in second place?

c. To the nearest thousandth of a kilometer per minute, how much faster was the swimming speed of the second-place finisher than the third-place finisher?

d. How much faster was the bike speed of the third-place finisher than her swimming speed? than her running speed?

Additional Practice (continued)

10. The table shows the populations and land areas of four towns. Population density is the ratio of population to land area. Find the population density for each town. Round to the nearest tenth.

Town	Population	Land Area (square miles)	Population Density (people per square mile)
Robins	3,345	5.8	
Highview	7,145	4.2	
Parkville	1,041	9.8	
Vernon	4,583	3.5	

11. The table shows the numbers of files and folder sizes for three folders on a computer.

   a. Find the average size for each type of file. Round to the nearest thousandth.

Folder Name	Number of Files	Total Folder Size (gigabytes)	Average File Size (gigabytes)
Pictures	1,458	14.64	
Music	230	1.6	
Movies	22	3.08	

   b. How many times greater is the average file size for a movie file compared to a music file?

   c. Rosa has 2,105 music files in a folder on her computer. What would you estimate the folder size in gigabytes to be? Explain your reasoning.

   d. A folder with pictures is 2.75 gigabytes. About how many files would you expect to find in the folder? Explain your reasoning.

Additional Practice: Digital Assessments

---

12. Katina walks 2.5 miles each morning. Eddy walks 3.1 miles each evening. Circle the numbers that make each statement true.

a. Katina walks
$\begin{bmatrix} 2.5 \\ 7.5 \\ 9.1 \\ 12.5 \\ 15.5 \end{bmatrix}$
miles after 5 days.

b. After 5 days, Eddy walks about

$\begin{bmatrix} 0.5 \\ 2.5 \\ 5.5 \end{bmatrix}$
miles more than Katina.

13. Erin bought four types of cheeses from a farmer's market. The table shows the type, weight, and cost of the cheese.

American	3 pounds	$12.87
Cheddar	2 pounds	$10.58
Muenster	1.5 pounds	$5.28
Swiss	4 pounds	$17.16

Which types of cheese cost a little more than $4 per pound? *Select all that apply.*

☐ American

☐ Cheddar

☐ Muenster

☐ Swiss

---

14. Using only the numbers and symbols on the tiles provided below, fill in each space to write an expression that can be used to solve each problem.

a. Julia, Tomas, and Lyn want to buy their friend a birthday present. Julia has $8.42, Tomas has $3.54, and Lyn has $6.51. How much money do they have altogether to purchase a present?

 3.54   6.51   8.42   +   −   ×   ÷

b. Kai's puppy, Shadow, received 3 vaccines at his first veterinarian appointment. One of the vaccines cost $10.25 and the other two cost $8.49 each. How much do the vaccines cost in all?

2   8.49   10.25   +   −   ×   ÷

Skill: Unit Rates

Determine the unit rates represented by each situation.

1. Zephra ran 2 miles in 0.25 hour.

2. It takes Toni 20 minutes to drive 5.2 miles to school.

3. A 2.5-pound bag of apples is priced at $5.59.

4. The curtain rod advertised has a length of 48 inches or 122 centimeters.

5. The bank exchanged 10 U.S. dollars for 8.84 euro.

6. Branson earned $61.33 for 5.5 hours of work.

7. The border on 3.5 scarves used 115.5 inches of ribbon.

8. The car traveled 311.6 miles on 19.0 gallons of gas.

Skill: Unit Rates (continued)

Use each unit rate to find a missing value.

9. There are about 1.6 kilometers per mile.

    a. How many kilometers are there in 60 miles?

    b. How many miles are there in 90.8 kilometers?

10. The price of a 1-square-foot tile is $4.89.

    a. How much do 112 tiles cost?

    b. How many tiles could be purchased for $500?

Skill: Unit Rates (continued)

11. The store multiplies its cost by 3.1 to determine the price of items.

    a. How much would the store charge for an item for which it paid $24.50?

    b. The price of an item at the store is $49.99. How much did the store pay for the item?

12. A smoothie recipe calls for 0.75 cup of berries for every 1 cup of yogurt and 1 cup of ice.

    a. How many cups of berries are needed for a 0.75-cup container of yogurt?

    b. There are 2.5 cups of berries. How much yogurt and ice is needed to make a smoothie using all the berries?

Additional Practice

1. James used a calculator to complete each computation. He forgot to write the decimal point in each answer. Write the correct answer for each computation.

Problem	Answer Without Decimal Point	Correct Answer
$5.7 + 6.09 + 4.2$	1599	
$3.007 - 2.9 + 35.054$	35161	
$14.5 - 8.07 - 6.2$	23	

2. Students used a computer program to test the time it took them to react to a green ball that appeared on a computer screen. Here are the reaction times for two students, a girl with initials LG and a boy with initials MC.

LG's data values:

Trial 1	Trial 2	Trial 3	Trial 4	Trial 5
1.08 sec	0.94 sec	0.64 sec	1.00 sec	0.94 sec

MC's data values:

Trial 1	Trial 2	Trial 3	Trial 4	Trial 5
1.25 sec	2.48 sec	1.15 sec	1.34 sec	1.47 sec

   a. Compute the difference in LG's and MC's data values for each trial.

   b. Find the sum of LG's data values.

   c. Find the sum of MC's data values.

   d. What are some statements you can make to compare the data from each of the two students?

Additional Practice *(continued)*

Find the value of n that makes each sentence true. Then write the addition and subtraction fact family for the sentence.

3. $2.3 + 4.09 = n$

4. $1.009 + 12.87 = n$

5. $19.81 - 12.25 = n$

6. $13.7 - 10.34 = n$

7. $n + 3.8 = 12.65$

8. $n - 2.4 = 5$

Additional Practice (continued)

Find the value of *n* that makes each sentence true. Then write the addition and subtraction fact family for the sentence.

9. $n + 8.4 = 15$

10. $n - 7.62 = 1.4$

11. $1.6 + n = 7.65$

12. $17.18 - n = 4.32$

Additional Practice: Digital Assessments

Decimal Operations

13. Which are in the fact family for $2.3 - n = 1.5$?
Select all that apply.

☐ $2.3 = 1.5 + n$
☐ $2.3 + n = 1.5$
☐ $n - 2.3 = 1.5$
☐ $2.3 = n + 1.5$
☐ $1.5 - n = 2.3$

14. Circle the number that makes each statement true.

a. $15.5 + \begin{bmatrix} 4.73 \\ 5.37 \\ 5.73 \\ 15.23 \\ 37.73 \end{bmatrix} = 21.23$

b. $2.3 + 12.64 + 8.281 = \begin{bmatrix} 9.568 \\ 9.775 \\ 11.845 \\ 22.121 \\ 23.221 \end{bmatrix}$

15. Shade and label the circles to show the correct location of each decimal on the number line.

| 1.3 | 1.08 | 1.75 | 1.5 | 1.11 | 1.89 |

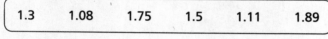

1.0   2.0

16. Order the decimals from smallest to largest.

4.3	4.303	4.03
4.33	4.033	4.003

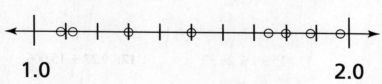

☐ , ☐ , ☐ , ☐ , ☐ , ☐

Skill: Adding and Subtracting Decimals

First estimate. Then find each sum or difference.

1. $0.6 + 5.8$

2. $2.1 + 3.4$

3. $3.4 - 0.972$

4. $3.1 - 2.076$

5. $8.13 - 2.716$

6. $5.91 + 2.38$

7. $3.086 + 6.152$

8. $4.7 - 1.9$

9. $9.3 - 3.9$

10. $5.2 - 1.86$

11. $15.98 + 26.37$

12. $9.27 + 15.006$

13. $5.9 - 2.803$

14. $15.7 - 8.923$

15. $4.19 - 2.016$

16. $14.75 - 6.9264$

17. $5.1 + 4.83 + 9.002$

18. $3 + 4.02 + 8.6$

Skill: Adding and Subtracting Decimals (continued)

Order each set of decimals on a number line.

19. 0.2, 0.6, 0.5

20. 0.26, 0.3, 0.5, 0.59, 0.7

Use the table at the right for Exercise 21–23.

21. Find the sum of the decimals given in the chart. What is the meaning of this sum?

Age of Workers Earning Hourly Pay

Age of Workers	Part of Work Force
16–19	0.08
20–24	0.15
25–34	0.29
35–44	0.24
45–54	0.14
55–64	0.08
65 & over	0.02

22. What part of the hourly work force is ages 25–44?

23. Which three age groups combined represent about one-fourth of the hourly work force?

Find the missing numbers.

24.
```
   12.84
 +    n
  30.123
```

25.
```
       n
 − 23.572
   41.617
```

26. $n - 16.321 = 20.2$

27. $3.02 + n - 6.1 = 12.74$

Additional Practice

1. Josh and his father are estimating how much gas they will need for a car trip. They know that the car gets 39 miles per gallon. Estimate how many gallons of gas they will need for a trip of 778 miles. Explain your reasoning.

2. The diagram below shows a rectangular plot of land cut into squares of 2.65 acres each.

   a. What is the acreage of the shaded region?

   b. What is the acreage of the unshaded region?

   c. In this area, land sells for $2,475 per acre.
      i. What would the price of the shaded region be?

      ii. What would the price of the unshaded region be?

   d. In this area, owners pay property taxes of $13.50 per thousand dollars of property value. What is the total annual property tax for the shaded and unshaded regions combined? Show your work.

3. Use the number sentence $123 \times 4 = 492$ to help you solve the following:
   a. 12.3×4
   b. 1.23×4
   c. 0.123×4

   d. 0.123×40
   e. 0.123×400
   f. 0.123×4000

Additional Practice (continued)

4. Use the number sentence $63 \times 501 = 31{,}563$ to help you solve the following:

   a. 6.3×5.01

   b. 6.3×0.501

   c. 6.3×50.1

   d. 0.63×5.01

   e. 0.63×501

   f. 0.63×0.501

5. Estimate each product. Explain.

   a. 2.4×0.8

   b. 5.21×1.1

   c. 1.29×8

6. For (a)–(c) in Exercise 5 above, find the product. Show your work.

7. Compute each product. What patterns do you notice?

   a. 5.5×9.9

   b. 5.5×9.99

   c. 5.5×9.999

   d. 5.5×9.9999

Additional Practice (continued)

8. Jason and his mother are re-tiling the kitchen floor. The area of the kitchen floor is 96.75 square feet. Each tile has an area of 1.25 square feet. How many tiles will Jason and his mother need to tile the kitchen?

9. The student concession stand buys 6.5 pounds of unpopped popcorn for $12.75. What is the price per pound of the popcorn?

10. For each of the following, decide if the quotient is less than 1 or greater than 1.

   a. $9.22 \div 2.8$ **b.** $0.9 \div 0.3$ **c.** $12.6 \div 11.8$ **d.** $5.6 \div 9.9$

11. Compute each quotient. What patterns do you notice?

   a. $6.3 \div 9$, $6.3 \div 0.9$, $6.3 \div 0.09$, $6.3 \div 0.009$

   b. $6.3 \div 9$, $0.63 \div 9$, $0.063 \div 9$, $0.0063 \div 9$

   c. $6.3 \div 9$, $0.63 \div 0.9$, $0.063 \div 0.09$, $0.0063 \div 0.009$

Additional Practice (continued)

12. Use the number sentence $936 \div 12 = 78$ to help you solve the following:

    a. $936 \div 1.2$ **b.** $93.6 \div 12$ **c.** $9.36 \div 12$

    d. $0.936 \div 12$ **e.** $936 \div 0.12$ **f.** $936 \div 0.012$

13. Use the number sentence $492 \div 4 = 123$ to help you solve the following:

    a. $492 \div 40$ **b.** $492 \div 400$ **c.** $492 \div 4000$

    d. $49.2 \div 4$ **e.** $4.92 \div 4$ **f.** $0.492 \div 4$

14. Find each quotient.

    a. $4.5 \div 0.3$ **b.** $64.4 \div 0.04$ **c.** $12.9 \div 20$

    d. $12.9 \div 0.2$ **e.** $1.05 \div 2.1$ **f.** $18.8 \div 4$

Additional Practice: Digital Assessments

Decimal Operations

15. Place a decimal point in the appropriate place in the product.

a. $0.64 \times 0.2 =$

$$0 \quad 1 \quad 2 \quad 8$$

b. $1.06 \times 10.4 =$

$$0 \quad 1 \quad 1 \quad 0 \quad 2 \quad 4$$

c. $3.54 \div 0.006 =$

$$0 \quad 0 \quad 5 \quad 9 \quad 0 \quad 0$$

16. Circle the number that makes the statement true.

a. $4.32 \div 1.8 = \begin{bmatrix} 0.42 \\ 2.4 \\ 2.52 \\ 6.12 \\ 7.776 \end{bmatrix}$

b. $0.64 \times 1.25 = \begin{bmatrix} 0.512 \\ 0.61 \\ 0.8 \\ 1.89 \\ 1.95 \end{bmatrix}$

c. $2.1 \times 0.55 = \begin{bmatrix} 0.26 \\ 1.155 \\ 1.55 \\ 2.65 \\ 3.81 \end{bmatrix}$

17. Write each expression in the appropriate box.

$3.25 \div 2.78$ $\qquad$ $2.81 \div 3.4$ $\qquad$ $5.1 \div 5.01$ $\qquad$ $1.25 \div 4.1$ $\qquad$ $5.2 \div 5.72$

Quotient Greater than 1	Quotient Less than 1

Name _____ Date _____ Class _____

Skill: Multiplying Decimals

Place the decimal point in each product.

1. $4.3 \times 2.9 = 1247$

2. $0.279 \times 53 = 14787$

3. $5.90 \times 6.3 = 3717$

Find each product.

4. 43.59×0.1

5. 246×0.01

6. 726×0.1

7. 5.342
$\times\ \ 13$

8. 0.19
$\times\ 0.05$

9. 6.4
$\times\ 0.09$

10. 240
$\times\ 0.02$

11. 43.79
$\times\ 42$

12. 0.72
$\times\ 0.43$

Skill: Multiplying Decimals (continued)

Use mental math to find each product.

13. 5.97×100

14. $4 \times 0.2 \times 5$

15. $3 \times (0.8 \times 1)$

16. 5.23×100

17. $0.38 \cdot 1{,}000$

18. $(5)(4.2) \times 10$

Write a number sentence you could use for each situation.

19. A pen costs $0.59. How much would a dozen pens cost?

20. A mint costs $0.02. How much would a roll of 10 mints cost?

21. A bottle of juice has a deposit of $0.10 on the bottle. How much deposit money would there be on 8 bottles?

22. An orange costs $0.09. How much would 2 dozen oranges cost?

Use <, =, or > to complete each statement.

23. $2.8 \times 10 \ \square \ 26 \cdot 100$

24. $38.6 \cdot 10 \ \square \ 2 \cdot 38.6 \cdot 5$

25. $3.1 \times 10 \ \square \ (0.5 \cdot 0.2)3.1$

26. $8.3 \cdot 10 \cdot 1 \ \square \ 8.3 \times 100$

Skill: Dividing Decimals

Use mental math to find each quotient.

1. $7.8 \div 10$

2. $8.91 \div 100$

3. $10\overline{)46.3}$

4. $0.6 \div 10$

5. $1.45 \div 10$

6. $62.3 \div 100$

Find each quotient.

7. $0.4 \div 0.02$

8. $3.9 \div 0.05$

9. $0.2\overline{)26}$

10. $0.4\overline{)1.08}$

11. $0.68 \div 0.2$

12. $0.02\overline{)0.06}$

13. $14\overline{)889}$

14. $0.09\overline{)0.108}$

15. $0.04\overline{)0.024}$

Use <, =, or > to complete each statement.

16. $56 \div 100 \ \square \ 5.6 \div 100$

17. $\$16.20 \div 10 \ \square \ \$162.00 \div 100$

Skill: Dividing Decimals (continued)

Find each quotient.

18. $1.8 \div 6$

19. $16\overline{)3.2}$

20. $17\overline{)5.1}$

21. $9\overline{)21.6}$

22. $15\overline{)123}$

23. $108 \div 5$

24. $50\overline{)17.5}$

25. $24\overline{)120.06}$

26. $9\overline{)11.24}$

Skill: Dividing Decimals (continued)

Solve.

27. A package of 25 mechanical pencils costs $5.75. How much does each pencil cost?

28. A sales clerk is placing books side by side on a shelf. She has 12 copies of the same book. If the books cover 27.6 inches of the shelf, how thick is each book?

29. The salt content in the Caspian Sea is 0.13 kilograms for every liter of water. How many kilograms of salt are in 70 liters?

Find each quotient. Identify each as a terminating or repeating decimal.

30. $2.5 \div 0.08$ **31.** $9.6 \div 0.5$ **32.** $0.25 \div 0.03$

Name _____ Date _____ Class _____

Additional Practice

1. For each item below find:
- the sales tax and
- the total cost of each item.

a. an $18 pair of gloves if the sales tax rate is 6.5%

b. $65 in party supplies if the sales tax rate is 8%

c. a $42 pair of shoes if the sales tax rate is 7.5%

d. a $0.75 apple if the sales tax rate is 7%

Additional Practice (continued)

2. Write and solve problems that could be represented by each percent bar below.

a.

b.

c.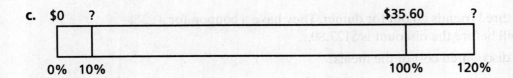

Additional Practice (continued)

3. Last Saturday, Aaron had lunch at a fast-food restaurant. He ordered the lunch special for $3.29. If sales tax is 6%, how much did Aaron pay for the lunch special?

4. Skateboards are on sale at Susan's Skateshop for 30% off.

   a. Express the discount as a fraction.

   b. If the regular price of a skateboard is $89, what is the discounted price?

   c. What is the total cost of the discounted skateboard in part (b) if sales tax is 4.5%?

5. Ms. Miller is charged $86 to get her hair cut and highlighted. If she wants to give the stylist a 15% tip, what is her total cost with tip?

6. Jacque and his three friends go out for dinner. They have a coupon for a 25% discount. The bill before the discount is $127.80.

   a. What is the discounted cost of the meals?

   b. After adding a 15% tip to the discounted cost, they divide the total equally. How much should each person pay? Round to the nearest cent.

Additional Practice: Digital Assessments

Decimal Operations

7. a. Shade the bar to represent 45% of 20.

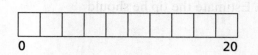

0   20

b. Shade the bar to represent 60% of 45.

0   45

8. The cost of a shirt is $16 and the shirt is 20% off. The tax rate is 5%. Circle the correct answer.

a. The price after the discount is $\begin{bmatrix} \$12.80 \\ \$13.44 \\ \$15.20 \\ \$16.80 \\ \$19.20 \end{bmatrix}$.

b. The price after tax is $\begin{bmatrix} \$12.80 \\ \$13.44 \\ \$16.25 \\ \$19.20 \\ \$20.00 \end{bmatrix}$.

9. Using only the numbers and symbols on the tiles provided below, fill in each box to write an expression.

Sally wrote an expression to find the total cost of a computer with a price of $450 and a tax rate of 7.5%. What could the expression have been?

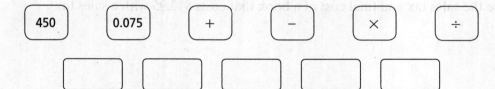

Skill: Using Percents

Solve by writing an equation.

1. Mr. Andropolis wants to leave the server a 12% tip. Estimate the tip he should leave if the family's bill is $32.46.

2. Michael buys a pair of jeans that regularly costs $62. The jeans were discounted by 80%. Estimate the discounted price of the jeans.

3. Estimate the sales tax and final cost of a book that costs $12.95 with a sales tax of 6%.

4. A real estate agent receives a 9% commission for every house sold. Suppose she sold a house for $212,000. Estimate her commission.

Skill: Using Percents (continued)

5. A jacket costs $94.95. It is on sale for 30% off. Estimate the sale price.

6. A restaurant offers a 13% discount on chicken wings on Mondays. On Friday, Travis eats $7.95 worth of chicken wings. How much would those wings cost on Monday?

7. Ian went out to dinner last night and remembers leaving a $6.50 tip. The tip was 20% of the cost of dinner. What was the cost of dinner before tip?

8. A store is selling a sweater on sale for $17.90. The regular price is $22.95. What percent of the regular price is the sale price?

Skill: Using Percents (continued)

Find each amount.

9. 40% of 70

10. 25% of 80

11. 50% of 80

12. 40% of 200

13. 5% of 80

14. 75% of 200

15. 14% of 120

16. 30% of 180

17. 62.5% of 24

Solve.

18. A farmer raised a watermelon that weighed 20 pounds. From his experience with raising watermelons, he estimated that 95% of the watermelon's weight is water.

   a. In pounds, how much of the watermelon is water?

   b. In pounds, how much of the watermelon is *not* water?

   c. The watermelon was shipped off to market. There it sat, until it had dehydrated (lost water). If the watermelon is still 90% water by weight, what percent of it is not water?

19. A bicycle goes on sale at 75% of its original price of $160. What is its sale price?

Additional Practice

1. a. The graph below shows the relationship between two variables. What are the variables?

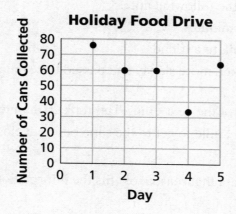

Holiday Food Drive

Number of Cans Collected (y-axis: 0, 10, 20, 30, 40, 50, 60, 70, 80)

Day (x-axis: 0, 1, 2, 3, 4, 5)

b. On which day were the most cans of food collected? About how many cans were collected on that day?

c. What total number of cans was collected over the 5 days? Explain your reasoning.

d. On this graph, does it make sense to connect the points with line segments? Explain your reasoning.

Additional Practice (continued)

2. Emma and her mother walk along a straight road from their house to their favorite ice cream shop. Emma keeps track of their pace over their seventy-five-minute walk. She made the following notes:

- We walked $\frac{3}{4}$ mile in the first 20 minutes.
- We stopped for 10 minutes to talk to a friend.
- For the next 20 minutes we walked more slowly and passed the $\frac{1}{2}$ mile of lovely gardens.
- We walked at our normal pace for the next $\frac{3}{4}$ mile. This took 20 minutes.
- We walked very fast for the last $\frac{1}{2}$ mile to get to the shop before it closed. This took only 5 minutes.

a. Make a table of (*time, distance*) data that reasonably fits the information in Emma's notes.

b. Sketch a coordinate graph that shows the same information as the table.

c. Does it make sense to connect the points on this graph? Explain your reasoning.

d. If Emma decided to only show one method of displaying the data (*time, distance*) to her mother, which should she choose if she wanted to show her mother the changes in their walking speed? Explain your choice.

Additional Practice (continued)

3. a. Andrew's mother kept the chart below of the number of words his sister Sarah could say at the end of each month from age 1 month to 24 months. Sarah did not say a word until 12 months, so from 1 to 11 Andrew's mother wrote 0. Make a coordinate graph of these data. Explain how you chose the variables for each axis.

Age (months)	Number of Words Sarah Can Say
1–11	0
12	1
13	1
14	2
15	3
16	7
17	10
18	15
19	24
20	28
21	30
22	47
23	51
24	62

b. Describe how the number of words Sarah can say changed as she got older (as the number of months passed).

c. During what month did Sarah learn to say the most words? The least (not counting from 1 to 11 months)?

Additional Practice (continued)

4. The Student Council of Metropolis Middle School voted on seven ideas related to school activities. There are nine students on the Student Council and each student voted "yes" or "no" for each idea. Use the information in the table at the right to answer parts (a)–(d).

   School Activity Ideas

Idea	Yes Votes
1	6
2	9
3	3
4	8
5	6
6	5
7	7

   a. What are the variables shown in the table?

   b. Which variable could be the independent variable and which could be the dependent variable? Explain your reasoning.

   c. Make a coordinate graph of the data in the table. Label your x-axis and y-axis with the correct independent or dependent variable.

   d. Make a coordinate graph showing how many students voted "no" on each of the seven ideas. Explain how you find the data for your graph. Label the x-axis and y-axis with the appropriate independent or dependent variable.

Name _____ Date _____ Class _____

Additional Practice (continued)

5. Below is a chart of the water depth in a harbor during a typical 24-hour day. The water level rises and falls with the tide.

Hours Since Midnight	0	1	2	3	4	5	6	7	8	9	10	11	12
Depth (meters)	8.4	8.9	9.9	10.7	11.2	12.1	12.9	12.2	11.3	10.6	9.4	8.3	8.0

Hours Since Midnight	13	14	15	16	17	18	19	20	21	22	23	24
Depth (meters)	8.4	9.4	10.8	11.4	12.2	13.0	12.4	11.3	10.4	9.8	8.6	8.1

a. Make a coordinate graph of the data.

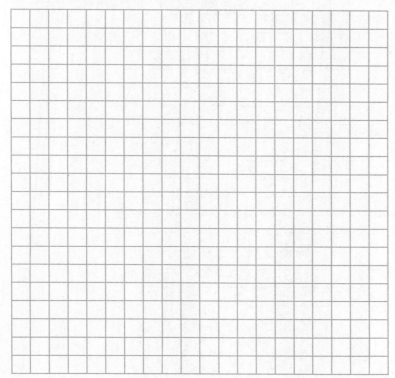

b. During which time interval(s) does the depth of the water increase the most?

c. During which time interval(s) does the depth of the water decrease the most?

d. Would it make sense to connect the points on the graph? Why or why not?

e. Is it easier to use the table or the graph to answer parts (b) and (c)? Explain.

Additional Practice (continued)

6. Make a table and a graph of (*time, temperature*) data that fit the following information about a day on the road:

- We started riding at 9:00 A.M. once the fog had burned off. The day was quite cool. The temperature was 52°F, and the sun was shining brightly.

- About midmorning, the temperature rose to 70°F and cloud cover moved in, which kept the temperature steady until lunch time.

- Suddenly the sun burst through the clouds, and the temperature began to climb. By late afternoon, it was 80°F.

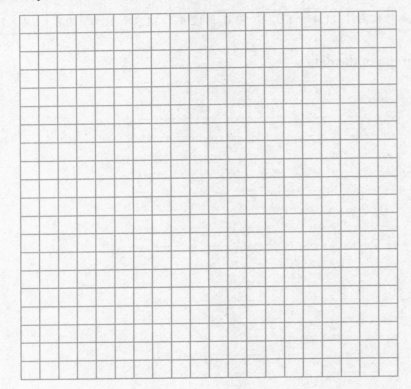

Additional Practice (continued)

7. Make a graph that shows your hunger level over the course of a day. Label the x-axis from 6 A.M. to midnight. Write a story about what happened during the day in relation to your hunger level.

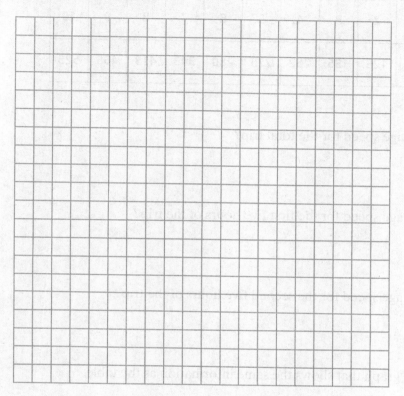

Additional Practice (continued)

8. The following table shows (*time, distance*) data for a ten-hour drive that Mr. and Ms. Shah took from Cleveland, Ohio, to Nashville, Tennessee.

Time (hours)	0	1	2	3	4	5	6	7	8	9	10
Distance (miles)	0	70	125	195	252	275	280	343	413	465	525

a. What was their average speed for the total trip?

b. What was their average speed for the first five hours of the trip?

c. What was their average speed for the second five hours of the trip?

d. Sketch a coordinate graph that shows the same information as the table.

e. What hour(s) of the trip did the Shahs travel the shortest distance? Travel the farthest?

f. Suppose the average speed of the final hour had been the average speed throughout the entire trip. Then how long would the trip have taken them?

Additional Practice: Digital Assessments

9. Carl rides his bike in a 12-hour cross-country race. The chart shows the total distance he rides by each hour mark.

Hours	0	1	2	3	4	5	6	7	8	9	10	11	12
Distance (miles)	0	14	26	35	47	51	57	64	77	85	94	101	116

a. Plot points on the coordinate grid to show the data from the chart.

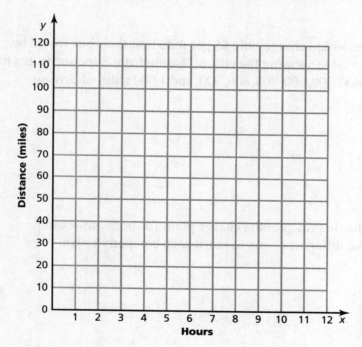

Circle the intervals that make each statement true.

b. Carl's fastest average speed is between hours $\begin{bmatrix} 0 \text{ and } 1 \\ 3 \text{ and } 4 \\ 4 \text{ and } 5 \\ 10 \text{ and } 11 \\ 11 \text{ and } 12 \end{bmatrix}$.

c. Carl's slowest average speed is between hours $\begin{bmatrix} 0 \text{ and } 1 \\ 4 \text{ and } 5 \\ 5 \text{ and } 6 \\ 10 \text{ and } 11 \\ 11 \text{ and } 12 \end{bmatrix}$.

Additional Practice

1. When the *Ocean Bike Tour* operators considered leasing a small bus for the summer season, they checked prices from two companies.

a. East Coast Transport (ECT) would charge $1,000 plus $2.50 per mile that their bus would be driven. Make a table showing the cost of leasing from ECT for 100, 200, 300, 400, 500, 600, 700, 800, 900, and 1,000 miles of driving.

b. Superior Buses would charge only $5 per mile that their bus would be driven. Make a table showing the cost of leasing from Superior Buses for 100, 200, 300, 400, 500, 600, 700, 800, 900, and 1,000 miles of driving.

c. On one coordinate grid, plot the charge plans for both bus-leasing companies. Use different colors to mark each company's plan.

d. Why, if at all, does it make sense to connect the dots on your plots of part (c)?

e. Based on your work in parts (a)–(c), which lease option seems best? How is your answer supported by data in the tables and patterns in the graphs?

Additional Practice (continued)

2. a. A newspaper included the graph below in a story about the amount of city land used for trash between 2000 and 2005. The graph shows the relationship between two variables. What are they?

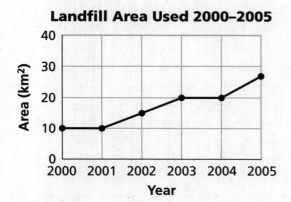

Landfill Area Used 2000–2005

b. What is the difference between the least and greatest amount of land used for trash?

c. Between which two years did the area used for trash stay the same?

d. On this graph, what information is given by the lines connecting the points? Is this information necessarily accurate? Explain your reasoning.

e. In 2000, the total area available for trash was 120 square kilometers. Make a coordinate graph that shows the landfill area remaining in each year from 2000 to 2005.

Additional Practice *(continued)*

3. a. Make a coordinate graph of these data.

Roller Rink Fees

Minutes	Cost
30	$3.50
60	$7.00
90	$10.50
120	$14.00
150	$17.50
180	$21.00

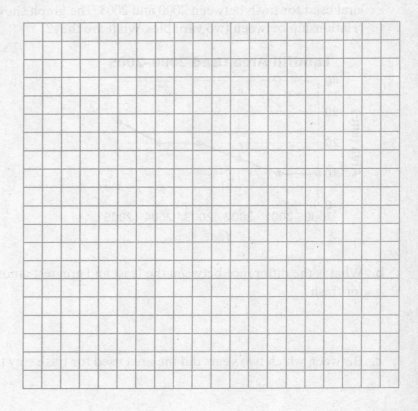

b. Would it make sense to connect the points on your graph? Why or why not?

c. Using the table, describe the pattern of change in the total skating fee as the number of minutes increases. How is this pattern shown in the graph?

Additional Practice (continued)

4. a. A roller-blade supply store rents roller blades for $2.50 per skater. Using increments of 5 skaters, make a table showing the total rental charge for 0 to 50 skaters. Make a coordinate graph of these data.

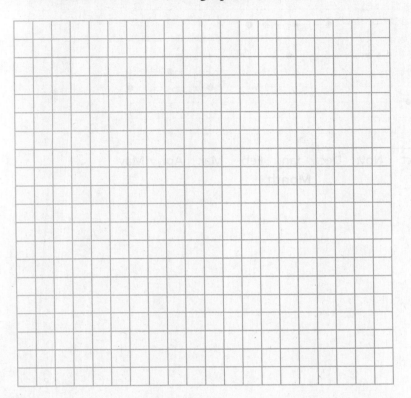

b. Compare the pattern of change in your table and graph with the patterns you found in the skating fees in Exercise 3. Describe any similarities and differences.

Additional Practice (continued)

5. a. Use the graph to make a table of data showing the sales for each month.

Roller Rink Concession Stand Sales

b. The profit made by the concession stand is half of the sales. Make a table of data that shows the profit made by the concession stand for each month.

Additional Practice *(continued)*

c. Make a coordinate graph of the data from part (b). Use the same scale used in the sales graph above. Describe how the sales graph and the profit graph are similar and how they are different.

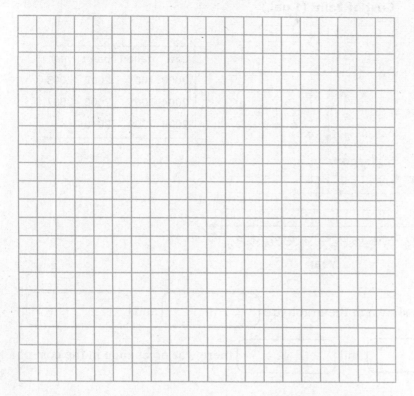

6. The three graphs below show the progress of a cyclist at different times during a ride. For each graph, describe the rider's progress over the time interval.

a.

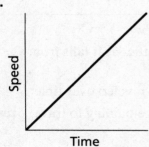

b.

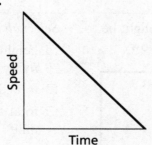

c.

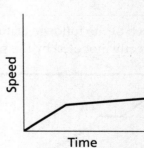

Additional Practice: Digital Assessments

7. The graph below shows the relationship between two variables.

Use the words and numbers in the bank to complete each statement.

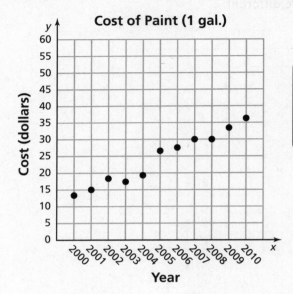

Cost of Paint (1 gal.)

cost	gallon	paint	year
2000	2001	2002	2003
2004	2005	2006	2007
2008	2009	2010

a. The two variables shown in the graph are [ ] and [ ].

b. Between [ ] and [ ] there was no change in the cost of a gallon of paint.

c. Between [ ] and [ ] the cost of a gallon of paint had the greatest increase.

8. Which of the following situations might be correctly modeled by the graph below?

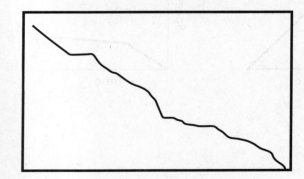

Select all that apply.

☐ height of a feather as it falls from a flying bird

☐ total distance traveled over time

☐ total distance remaining to travel over time

☐ path of a basketball through a hoop

☐ snow accumulation during a blizzard

Skill: Tables and Graphs

1. a. Graph the data in the table.

Storage Disks

Number of disks	Price (dollars)
1	20
2	37
3	50
6	100
10	150

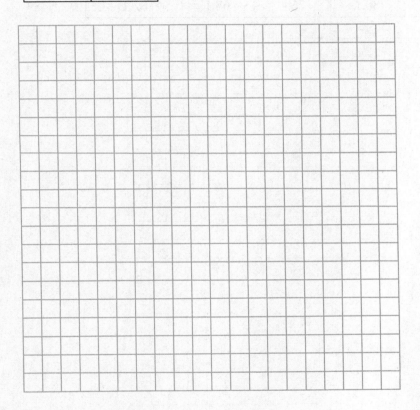

b. Use the graph to estimate the cost of five disks.

Skill: Tables and Graphs *(continued)*

2. a. The table shows average monthly temperatures in degrees Fahrenheit for
American cities in January and July. Graph the data in the table.

City	Seattle	Baltimore	Boise	Chicago	Dallas	Miami	LA
Jan.	39.1	32.7	29.9	21.4	44.0	67.1	56.0
Jul.	64.8	76.8	74.6	73.0	86.3	82.5	69.0

City	Anchorage	Honolulu	New York	Portland	New Orleans
Jan.	13.0	72.6	31.8	21.5	52.4
Jul.	58.1	80.1	76.4	68.1	82.1

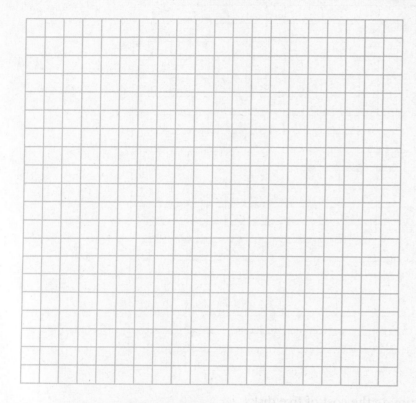

b. Use your graph to estimate the July temperature of a city whose average
January temperature is 10°F.

Name _____ Date _____ Class _____

Skill: Analyzing Graphs

Graphs I through VI represent one of the six situations described below. Match each graph with the situation that describes it.

I. 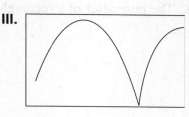   II. 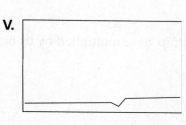   III.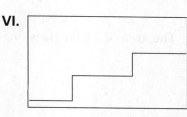

IV. 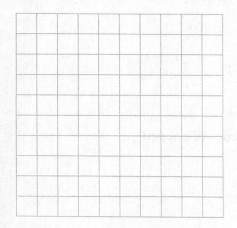   V. 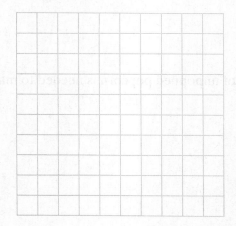   VI.

1. temperature as the weather changes from rainy to snowy

2. number of fish caught per hour on a bad fishing day

3. total rainfall during a rainy day

4. speed of a car starting from a stop sign and then approaching a stoplight

5. height of a cricket as it jumps

6. total amount of money spent over time during a trip to the mall

Sketch a graph for each situation.

7. The speed of a runner in a 1-mi race.

8. The height above ground of the air valve on a tire of a bicycle ridden on flat ground. (You can model this using a coin.)

Additional Practice

1. In parts (a)–(e), use symbols to express the rule as the equation. Use single letters to stand for the variables. Identify what each letter represents.

   a. The perimeter of a rectangle is twice its length plus twice its width.

   b. The area of a triangle is one-half its base multiplied by its height.

   c. Three big marshmallows are needed to make each s'more.

   d. The number of quarters in an amount of money expressed in dollars is four times the number of dollars.

   e. A half-cup of unpopped popcorn is needed to make 6 cups of popped popcorn.

Additional Practice (continued)

2. The equation $d = 44t$ represents the distance in miles covered, after traveling 44 miles per hour for t hours.

   a. Make a table that shows the distance traveled, according to this equation, for every half hour between 0 and 4 hours.

   b. Sketch a graph that shows the distance traveled between 0 and 4 hours.

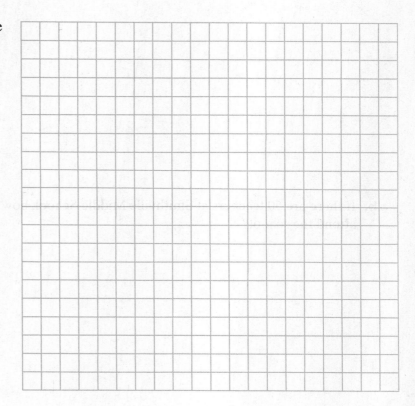

   c. If $t = 2.5$, what is d?

   d. If $d = 66$, what is t?

   e. Does it make sense to connect the points on this graph with line segments? Why or why not?

Additional Practice (continued)

3. a. The number of students at Smithville Middle School is 21 multiplied by the number of teachers. Use symbols to express the rule relating the number of students and the number of teachers as an equation. Use single letters for your variables and explain what each letter represents.

b. If there are 50 teachers at Smithville Middle School, how many students attend the school?

c. If 1,260 students attend Smithville Middle School, how many teachers teach at the school?

Additional Practice (continued)

4. a. Refer to the table below. Use symbols to express the rule relating the side length of a square to its area as an equation. Use single letters for your variables, and explain what each letter represents.

Squares

Side Length (cm)	Area (cm²)
1	1
1.5	2.25
2	4
2.5	6.25
3	9

b. Use your equation to find the area of a square with a side length of 6 centimeters.

c. Use your equation to find the side length of a square with an area of 1.44 square centimeters.

Additional Practice: Digital Assessments

5. Which of the following input-output pairs follow the rule?

Rule: Output = Input • 3

Select all that apply.

☐ For an input of 6, the output is 18.

☐ Input = 3
Output = 1

☐ An input of 4 has an output of 12.

☐ When the input is 2, the output is 10.

☐ Input = 5
Output = 10

☐ Input = 1
Output = 3

6. Using the numbers on the tiles, complete the table.

| 2 | 8 | 12 | 15 |

| 20 | 30 | 32 | 40 |

x	$2.5x$
4	10
	20
12	
16	
	50

7. Match each situation to an equation.

Two batches of muffins use 5 cups of flour.

$5x = 2y$

The number of feet in a distance expressed in yards is three times the number of yards.

$y = 5 + 2x$

1 cup of juice concentrate is needed to make 5 quarts of punch.

$y = 5x$

The cost of going to the county fair is a $5-entrance fee and $2 per ride.

$x = 3y$

Skill: Variables, Tables, and Graphs

In programming, an input can be thought of as the independent variable. An output can be thought of as the dependent variable. Complete each table given the rule.

1. Rule: Input · 5 = Output

Input	1	2	3	4	5
Output	5	10	15		

2. Rule: Input · 2 = Output

Input	10	20	30	40	50
Output	20	40	60		

3. Rule: Input + 3 = Output

Input	3	4	5	6	7
Output	6	7	8		

4. Rule: Input + 1 = Output

Input	6	7	8	9	10
Output	7	8	9		

5. Rule: Input − 4 = Output

Input	12	13	14	15	16
Output	8	9	10		

Skill: Variables, Tables, and Graphs (continued)

6. A parking garage charges $3.50 per hour to park. The equation $c = 3.5h$ shows how the number of hours h relates to the parking charge c. Graph this relationship.

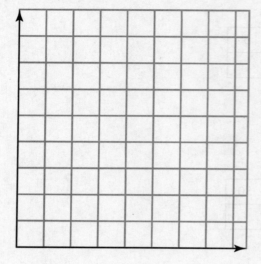

Use the expression to complete each table.

7.

x	x + 7
2	9
5	12
8	
11	
	21

8.

x	5x
3	
6	
9	
12	
	75

9.

x	125 − x
15	
30	
45	
60	
	50

Skill: Variables, Tables, and Graphs (continued)

10. A cellular phone company charges a $49.99 monthly fee for 600 free minutes. Each additional minute costs $0.35. This month you used 750 minutes. How much do you owe?

Write a rule for the relationship between the variables represented in each table.

11.

x	y
1	6
2	7
3	8
4	9

12.

x	y
1	4
2	8
3	12
4	16

13.

x	y
1	4
2	7
3	10
4	13

14. A typist types 45 words per minute.

   a. Write a rule to represent the relationship between the number of typed words and the time in which they are typed.

   b. How many words can the typist type in 25 minutes? Write and solve an equation to answer this.

   c. How long would it take the typist to type 20,025 words?

Name _____ Date _____ Class _____

Additional Practice

Variables and Patterns

Use the shape pattern to complete Exercises 1 and 2.

 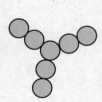 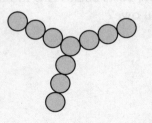 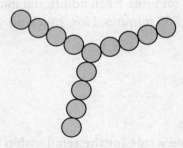

Shape 1   **Shape 2**   **Shape 3**   **Shape 4**

1. **a.** Complete the table comparing the shape number to the number of circles.

Shape Number	4	5	6	7	8	10	20
Number of Circles	13						

   b. Write an equation that could be used to find the number of circles C needed for shape number n. Explain how your equation relates to the shape pattern.

   c. How many circles are needed for shape number 40? Explain how you found your answer.

   d. What shape number requires 28 circles? Explain how you found your answer.

Additional Practice (continued)

2. a. Grace wrote the equation $C = 4n$ to represent the shape pattern. Is Grace's equation correct? Explain how Grace might have arrived at her equation.

b. Write a different equation from Exercise 1(b) that represents the shape pattern.

c. Show that the two equations are equivalent.

Additional Practice *(continued)*

Use the information to complete Exercises 3 and 4.

Brandon is constructing a garden using the side of the house as a wall. He isn't sure how long to make the garden. Here are sketches of three designs using 1-foot square tiles to surround the three sides of the garden.

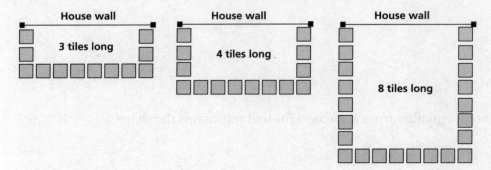

3. a. Complete the table comparing the length to the number of tiles needed to surround it.

Length of Garden in Tiles	3	4	5	6	7	8	10	20
Number of Tiles Needed	12	14						

b. What is an equation you can use to find the number of tiles F needed for a garden that is n tiles long?

c. Could you calculate the number of tiles needed for a garden that is 1 tile long? Explain.

4. Brandon and his friends wrote equations to represent the number of tiles needed for a garden that is n feet wide. Which equations represent the pattern?

Brandon's equation: $F = 8 + n + n$

Linda's equation: $F = 2n + 6$

Alex's equation: $F = 8 + 2(n - 1)$

Additional Practice (continued)

Use the information and table to complete Exercises 5–7.

A mini-golf course offers a birthday party package. The different options of the package are shown in the table.

Option	Cost
Room Reservation	$25
Mini-Golf	$3 per guest
Pizza and Drinks	$5 per guest
10 Tokens	$2 per guest
Birthday Cake	$25

5. Write an expression that shows the cost of each item for the number n of guests who attend a birthday party.

   a. Room reservation

   b. Mini golf

   c. Pizza, cake, and drinks

   d. Game tokens

6. a. Write a rule that shows how the cost C depends on the number n of guests who attend a birthday party with every option in the package. This rule should show how each package option adds to the total cost.

   b. Write another rule for the total package cost C. This rule should be as simple as possible for calculating the total cost. Give evidence that this rule is equivalent to the rule you wrote in part (a).

7. a. How much does the party package with all the options cost if 8 guests attend the party?

   b. If the budget for a party is $200, how many guests can attend the party? Write and solve an inequality that represents this situation.

Additional Practice *(continued)*

8. Jamie has 12 inches of bendable wire. She wants to use the wire to form two sides of a triangular frame. Part of a 6-inch stick will form the third side with length a as shown.

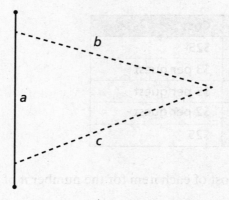

   a. Write an equation that represents how to find the perimeter P of the triangle above.

   b. Write an equation that represents how sides b and c are related to the length of the bendable wire.

   c. If the two ends of the wire are glued to the two ends of the stick, what is the perimeter of the triangle? Write an equation to represent this perimeter. Can the perimeter be greater than this? Why or why not?

   d. Write an inequality to solve for possible values of a.

Additional Practice *(continued)*

9. A painter charges $200 for materials and $40 per hour for painting a house. He charged the Fishers $400 for painting their house. Write and solve an equation to show how many hours the painter worked.

The library book fair charges a $5 entry fee and $1 per book. A school book fair charges $2 per book. Use this information for Exercises 10–13.

10. For each book fair, write an equation to show how total cost C depends on the number b of books purchased.

11. Henry spent $17 at the library book fair.

a. Write and solve an equation to show how many books Henry purchased.

b. Explain how you found your solution.

c. Check your solution by substituting its value for b in the equation.

Additional Practice (continued)

12. Lucy spent $12 at the school book fair.

   a. Write and solve an equation to show how many books Lucy purchased.

   b. Explain how you found your solution.

   c. Check your solution by substituting its value for b in the equation.

13. a. Parker has $10 to spend. Write and solve an equation to show the most books he can purchase at the library book fair.

   b. Parker has $10 to spend. Write and solve an equation to show the most books he can purchase at the school book fair.

   c. Which book fair do you think Parker should attend? Explain your reasoning.

Additional Practice (continued)

Use what you know about variables, expressions, and equations to write and solve inequalities that match exercises 14–16. In each case, do the following:

   a. **Write an inequality that helps to answer the question.**

   b. **Give at least 3 specific number solutions to the inequality. Then explain why they work.**

   c. **Describe all possible solutions.**

14. Belinda is constructing a square garden. What are the possible side lengths of the garden if she can use up to 60 feet of fencing?

15. Geoff bought a shelf that will fit 100 DVDs. If Geoff already has 27 DVDs, how many more can he purchase that will fit on the shelf?

16. A large cheese pizza costs $12.50 and each additional topping costs $1. How many toppings can Max order if he has $16.00 to spend on a pizza?

Additional Practice (continued)

17. Solve each inequality. Draw a number line and graph each solution.

    a. $m \div 5 < 8$

    b. $24 - w > 13$

    c. $4.5 + x > 5.75$

    d. $2.5 < 0.5n$

Additional Practice: Digital Assessments

Variables and Patterns

18. Which of the following number lines represents the solution to $1.5k < 6$?

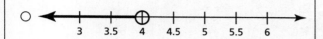

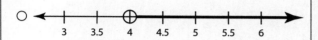

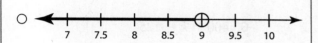

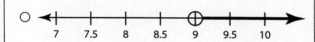

19. A ski shack offers special pricing on group rentals for a four-hour session and meals. The prices for each option are listed in the table.

Option	Cost
Skis	$30 per person
Snowboard	$35 per person
Boots	$10 per person
Meal ticket	$7 per person
XL Whole pizza	$12

Use the tiles to write an expression for each of the following options for a group size of n:

| $7n$ | $10n$ | 12 | $30n$ | $35n$ |

| $+$ | $-$ |

a. Skis

[   ]

b. Snowboards and an XL pizza

[   ]

c. Skis, boots, and meal tickets

[   ]

20. For the inequality $y - 3.5 > 7.1$, determine which values are solutions. Write each value in the box with the correct category.

$y = 11.2$ $y = 3.5$ $y = 10.6$ $y = -2.4$ $y = 2.9$ $y = 12.7$

Solution	Not a Solution

Skill: Finding Solutions

Variables and Patterns

Solve.

1. $x + 16 = 31$ **2.** $4.8 = 2.1 + c$ **3.** $m + 147 = 207$

4. $29 - k = 12$ **5.** $p - 4.1 = 2.2$ **6.** $400 = k - 125$

7. $9a = 72$ **8.** $3.6 = 0.6x$ **9.** $10p = 245$

10. $y \div 8 = 11$ **11.** $7.5 \div g = 1.5$ **12.** $n \div 30 = 13$

Skill: Finding Solutions (continued)

For each inequality, determine which values are solutions.

13. $k + 2.4 < 5.2$

    a. $k = 2$ **b.** $k = 2.8$ **c.** $k = 3.1$

14. $8.4 - x > 3.1$

    a. $x = 4.5$ **b.** $x = 5.2$ **c.** $x = 5.6$

15. $63 < 7p$

    a. $p = 7$ **b.** $p = 8.5$ **c.** $p = 9.1$

16. $d \div 3 > 5$

    a. $d = 14$ **b.** $d = 18$ **c.** $d = 20$

Additional Practice

1. Ms. Snow's students wrote down a whole number between 1 and 10 on a slip of paper. She collected the numbers and displayed the data in the dot plot below.

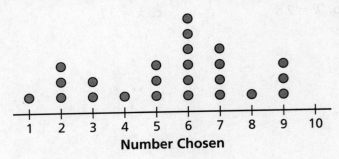

Number Chosen

   a. What is the typical number chosen by students in this class?

   b. Two students were absent on the day Ms. Snow collected the data. How many students are enrolled in the class? Explain your reasoning.

2. Mr. Watkins arranged the quiz scores of his afternoon math class from least to greatest: 5, 5, 6, 6, 6, 7, 7, 7, 7, 7, 8, 8, 8, 8, 8, 8, 9, 9, 9, 10, 10

   a. How many students are in Mr. Watkins's afternoon math class?

   b. How do the quiz scores vary?

   c. What is the mode of the scores?

   d. What is the median of the scores?

Additional Practice (continued)

3. The students in Mr. Furgione's math class counted the letters in the names of the streets where they lived. Then they made the bar graph below.

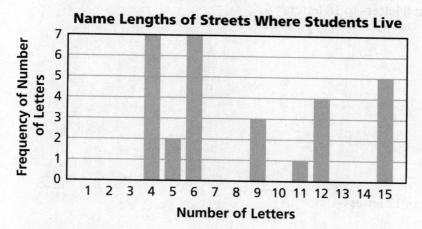

Name Lengths of Streets Where Students Live

a. Use the bar graph to make a table showing each name length and the number of students who live on streets with names of that length. Then make a dot plot showing these name lengths.

b. Nobody was absent when the data were collected. How many students are in Mr. Furgione's class? Explain your reasoning.

c. What is the typical street-name length for this class? Use the mode, median, and range to help you answer this question.

Additional Practice (continued)

For Exercises 4–7, make a frequency table and either a dot plot or a bar graph of a set of name-length data that fits the description.

4. 24 names that vary from 6 letters to 18 letters

5. 9 names with a median of 12 letters

6. 11 names that vary from 6 to 15 letters and a median of 13 letters

7. 14 names with a median of 12 letters and a range of 7 letters to 17 letters

Additional Practice (continued)

8. Mr. Wanko's classroom looks out over one of the school's parking lots. His class made the bar graph below of the colors of the vehicles parked in the lot.

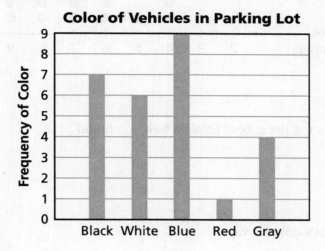

Color of Vehicles in Parking Lot

a. Make a frequency table to show the same information as the bar graph.

b. How many vehicles are parked in the lot?

c. Which vehicle color seems most popular? Explain.

d. Suppose Mr. Wanko's class collected data on the colors of vehicles parked in the same lot next week and represented the data in a bar graph. Would you expect this new bar graph to be the same as the one above? Why or why not?

Additional Practice *(continued)*

9. Edna rolled a pair of six-sided number cubes several times and recorded the sums on the dot plot at right.

   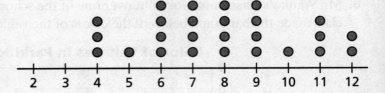

   a. Which roll(s) occurred most often? Explain your reasoning.

   b. How many times did Edna roll the cubes? Explain how you found your answer.

   c. How do the sums on Edna's dot plot vary?

   d. What is the median sum? Explain.

   e. Suppose you roll a pair of number cubes the same number of times as Edna did. Would you expect a dot plot of your results to look exactly like Edna's? Explain.

Use this dot plot for questions 10 and 11 below.

Name Lengths of Mr. Samuel's Students

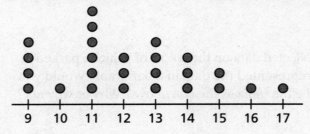

10. What is the median name length for this class?

    A. 13   **B.** 12   **C.** 11   **D.** 3

11. How do the name lengths for this class vary?

    F. 1 to 6   **G.** 9 to 17   **H.** 4 to 1   **J.** none of these

Additional Practice: Digital Assessments

12. Mr. Chen made a dot plot to show the number of books his students read over the summer. Use the dot plot to answer parts (a) and (b).

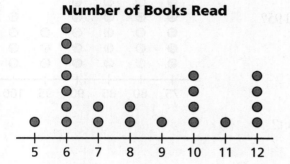

Number of Books Read

Circle the numbers and symbols that make each statement true.

a. The dot plot shows that $\begin{bmatrix} 4 \\ 5 \\ 13 \\ 17 \end{bmatrix}$ students read fewer than 10 books over the summer.

b. Most students read $\begin{bmatrix} 6 \\ 7 \\ 12 \\ 17 \end{bmatrix}$ books over the summer.

13. The dot plot shows the scores for the sixth-grade basketball teams. Use the dot plot to answer parts (a) and (b).

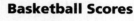

Basketball Scores

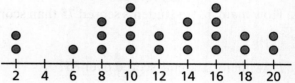

Complete the statements using the values from the bank.

> 2 6 10 20 22 23 24 25

a. The basketball teams played a total of ☐ games.

b. The scores vary from ☐ to ☐.

14. Ms. Janice recorded her students' test scores in order from least to greatest: 75, 80, 80, 90, 90, 90, 90, 95, 95, 100, 100, 100. Which dot plot represents this data?

○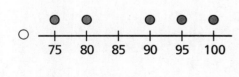

○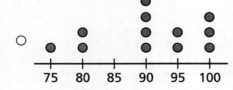

○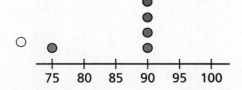

○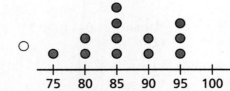

Skill: Dot Plots

Ms. Makita made a dot plot to show the scores her students got on a test. The dot plot is shown at the right.

1. What does each data item or ● represent?

2. How many more students scored 75 than scored 95?

3. How many students scored over 85?

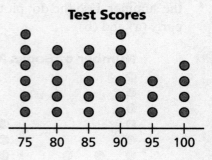

Test Scores

4. What scores did the same number of students get?

For Exercises 5–8, use the dot plot at the right.

5. What information is displayed in the dot plot?

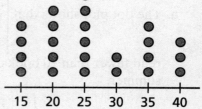

Time Spent Doing Homework Last Night (min)

6. How many students spent time doing homework last night?

7. How many students spent at least half an hour on homework?

8. How did the time spent on homework last night vary?

9. A kennel is boarding dogs that weigh the following amounts (in pounds).

| 5 | 62 | 43 | 48 | 12 | 17 | 29 | 74 |
| 8 | 15 | 4 | 11 | 15 | 26 | 63 | |

a. How do the dogs' weights vary?

b. How many of the dogs weigh under 50 pounds?

Additional Practice

1. The mean amount of change that Betty, Bill, and Susan have in their pockets is 79 cents. What is the total value of the change they have together? Explain.

2. Glenda rolled two six-sided number cubes nine times and computed the sum of the numbers rolled each time.

   a. If the mean sum of Glenda's rolls was 6, what was the total of the nine sums Glenda rolled?

   b. Suppose Glenda's rolls were 12, 7, 3, 10, 9, 2, 11, 7, and 8.
      i. What is the median of Glenda rolls?

      ii. What is the mean of Glenda's rolls?

      iii. What is the mode of Glenda's rolls?

      iv. Which do you think is the best indicator of a typical roll Glenda made, the median, mean, or mode? Explain your reasoning.

   c. Suppose Glenda rolled a total sum of 60 for her nine rolls.
      i. What is the mean sum for the rolls Glenda made?

      ii. Give an example of nine rolls that Glenda could have made. Explain.

Additional Practice (continued)

3. Mrs. Wilcox asked each of her students to spin a spinner with 12 equal sections labeled with whole numbers between 1 and 12. The dot plot shows the results of the students' spins.

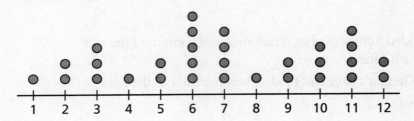

   a. How many students are in Mrs. Wilcox's class?

   b. What is the mean value of the spinner results by Mrs. Wilcox's class?

   c. What is the median value of the spinner results by Mrs. Wilcox's class?

   d. Which do you think is the better indicator of a typical result of a student's spin in Mrs. Wilcox's class, the median or the mean? Explain your reasoning.

4. The students in North Middle School had a contest to see who could save the most money. The mean savings in Ms. Jones' class (25 students) was the same as the mean savings for the whole school (300 students). The mean amount was $16.00.

   a. What is the total savings for Ms. Jones' students? Explain.

   b. What is the total savings for the whole school? Explain.

Name _____ Date _____ Class _____

Additional Practice (continued)

5. Every student in Mr. Smith's class tossed 3 coins and counted the number of heads. The bar graph below displays their results.

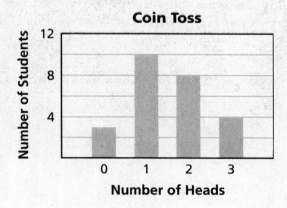

Coin Toss

a. How many students are in Mr. Smith's class?

b. What is the mean number of heads?

c. What is the median number of heads?

d. How many heads did the students toss altogether?

e. How many tails did the students toss altogether?

6. The Cycle Shoppe sells 10 brands of bicycles with these prices:
$90, $90, $110, $120, $120, $150, $150, $150, $180, $240

Biker's Haven sells 10 similar brands of bicycles with these prices:
$90, $100, $100, $100, $140, $150, $150, $170, $180, $250

  a. Make two dot plots, one for each bike shop. Use the same scale on each dot plot.

  b. What is the mean price for each bike shop?

  c. What is the median price for each bike shop?

  d. For each bike shop, which measure of central tendency seems to most accurately reflect the prices of the bikes? Explain.

Additional Practice (continued)

For Exercises 7 and 8, use this information.

    Mr. Johnson's class of 20 students collects 180 cans of food for the food drive.

    Ms. Smith's class of 25 students collects 200 cans of food.

7. Which class has a greater mean number of cans of food?

    A. Mr. Johnson's class   **B.** Ms. Smith's class

    C. The means are equal.   **D.** There isn't enough information to tell.

8. Which class has a greater median number of cans of food?

    F. Mr. Johnson's class   **G.** Ms. Smith's class

    H. The means are equal.   **J.** There isn't enough information to tell.

Additional Practice: Digital Assessments

9. The students in Ms. Allen's class collected aluminum cans for a recycling program. The numbers of cans collected per student were 10, 14, 10, 17, 11, 9, 3, 15, and 10.

Circle the numbers that make each statement true.

a. The median number of cans collected is $\begin{bmatrix} 10 \\ 11 \\ 14 \\ 20 \end{bmatrix}$.

b. The mean number of cans collected is $\begin{bmatrix} 10 \\ 11 \\ 14 \\ 20 \end{bmatrix}$.

c. The mode number of cans collected is $\begin{bmatrix} 10 \\ 11 \\ 14 \\ 20 \end{bmatrix}$.

10. The table shows the number of movie tickets sold over four days at different theaters.

Number of Movie Tickets Sold Over Four Days

Fun Time Theater	Royalty Cinema	Five Star Movies
508	356	490

Select *true* or *false* for each statement.

	true	false
The Fun Time Theater sold a mean number of 127 tickets per day.	○	○
There is not enough information to determine the mode for the number of tickets sold at Royalty Cinema.	○	○
There is not enough information to determine the mean number of tickets sold at all three theaters.	○	○

Skill: Mean, Median, and Mode

For Exercises 1–3, use the table.

1. What is the mean height of the active volcanoes listed to the nearest foot?

Active Volcanoes	
Name	**Height Above Sea Level (ft)**
Cameroon Mt.	13,354
Mount Erebus	12,450
Asama	8,300
Gerde	9,705
Sarychev	5,115
Ometepe	5,106
Fogo	9,300
Mt. Hood	11,245
Lascar	19,652

2. What is the median height of the active volcanoes listed?

3. What is the mode of the heights of the active volcanoes listed?

The sum of the heights of all the students in a class is 1,472 inches.

4. The mean height is 5 feet 4 inches. How many students are in the class? (1 ft = 12 in.)

5. The median height is 5 feet 2 inches. How many students are 5 feet 2 inches or taller? How many are shorter?

Skill: Mean, Median, and Mode (continued)

The number of pages read (to the nearest multiple of 50) by the students in history class last week are shown in the tally table.

Pages	50	100	150	200	250	300	350	400	450	500	550	600	650	700	750
Tally	I		II	⊬ I	I	⊬	III	IIII	I	I					I

6. Find the mean, the median, and the mode of the data.

7. Are there any outliers in this set of data?

8. Do any outliers raise or lower the mean?

9. Would you use the mean, median, or mode to most accurately reflect the typical number of pages read by a student? Explain.

Additional Practice

The members of a chess club sell raffle tickets to earn money for their activities.

1. On the first day, Paula records how much each person earned from selling tickets.

Chess Club Ticket Sales

Student	Paula	Quin	Robert	Stephanie
Amount	$13.25	$10.40	$15.65	$12.70

a. Find the range of the sales amounts.

b. The four chess club members share the sales equally. How much does each member receive?

c. The fifth member of the chess club, Tucker, brings his money in late. He brings $13.65. Paula then recalculates each person's share using all five members' earnings. Without doing any computation, how does this affect the amount each member receives? Explain.

2. On the second day, Tucker sold $18.50 in raffle tickets. After sharing the sales equally, each member's share was $11.45. What does this say about the Day 2 sales for the other four students? Explain.

Additional Practice *(continued)*

3. Kiaya and Kendrick are preparing for the long jump at a track meet. The long jumps are measured in meters.

Kiaya records the following jumps: 4.4, 5.0, 4.9, 5.1, 4.8, 4.8, 4.9, 4.9

Kendrick records the following jumps: 4.8, 4.7, 3.8, 5.3, 4.9, 4.8, 4.5, 5.2

a. Make a line plot of each person's jumps.

b. What are the median and IQR for each distribution?

c. What are the mean and MAD for each distribution?

d. At the track meet, who is more likely to make the longest jump? Explain your answer using measures of center and variability.

Additional Practice *(continued)*

4. Ben and Bob are learning to surf. Their mother times how many seconds the boys stand on their surfboards during each ride. The dot plots below show the distributions of ten surf times for each boy.

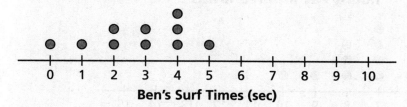

Ben's Surf Times (sec)

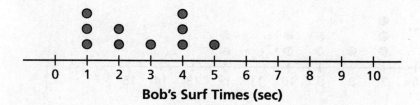

Bob's Surf Times (sec)

a. Find the mean of each data set.

b. Find the MAD of each data set.

c. Compare the MADs. In which distribution do the data vary more from the mean? Explain.

d. Bob's friend Brian is learning to surf. Ben records Brian's times, in seconds: 3, 3, 3, 4, 4, 4, 4, 5, 5, and 6.

   i. Draw a dot plot to show Brian's data.

   ii. Compute the MAD of Brian's data set.

   iii. Compare the three distributions. In which distribution do the data vary most from the mean? Explain your thinking.

For Exercises 5–7, use the line plots below. Each line plot shows the hourly pay
teenagers earn at similar jobs in different towns.

Hourly Pay in Three Towns

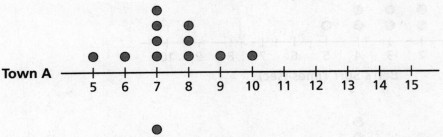

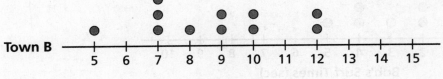

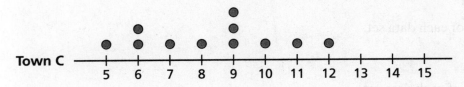

5. Find the interquartile range (IQR) and mean absolute deviation (MAD) of
   each data set.

6. Using the MAD, which distribution has the least variation from the mean?
   The most?

7. Using the IQR, which distribution has the greatest spread in the middle 50%
   of the data? The least?

Additional Practice (continued)

8. The frequency table shows the number of points scored by 3 players on the basketball team in 15 games.

Player's Points

Game	1	2	3	4	5	6	7	8	9	10	11	12	13	14	15
Player A	5	4	5	2	8	5	6	2	4	0	5	10	6	4	5
Player B	2	1	0	2	3	2	3	1	0	3	1	3	2	0	3
Player C	3	4	3	2	5	3	4	3	2	5	2	4	3	3	5

a. Draw a line plot or dot plot of each player's data. Use the same scale on each graph so you can easily compare the distributions.

b. Compute the median and IQR for each player. Write a statement that compares the players using the median and IQR.

c. Compute the mean and MAD for each player. Write a statement that compares the players using the mean and MAD.

Additional Practice: Digital Assessments

9. The dot plots show the number of goals made by two members of a soccer team for ten games.

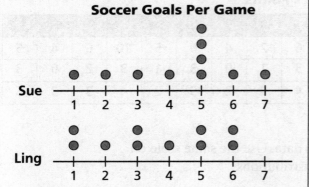

Soccer Goals Per Game

Which statements describe the data?

Select all that apply.

☐ Based on the mean of the data sets, Ling had a greater average number of goals per game.

☐ Based on the IQR, Sue's distribution had the greater spread in the middle 50% of the data.

☐ The MAD of Ling's data set is 1.6.

☐ The MAD of Sue's data set is 4.3.

☐ Based on the MAD of the data sets, Sue's distribution has the least variation from the mean.

10. Ryan and Ingrid earn money by mowing lawns. The dot plots show how much each of them earn per lawn in their neighborhoods.

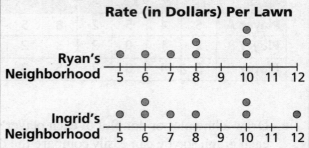

Rate (in Dollars) Per Lawn

Using the tiles provided, fill in the spaces to complete the statements.

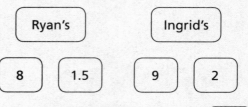

| Ryan's | Ingrid's |

| 8 | 1.5 | 9 | 2 |

a. The MAD of Ryan's data set is ☐.

b. The MAD of Ingrid's data set is ☐.

c. Based on the MAD, ☐ data distribution had the greater variation from the mean.

11. Ahmed and Sunil are in a math contest. They are completing math problems in a speed round. The dot plots show how many minutes they each spent completing ten math problems.

Circle the numbers and name that make each statement true.

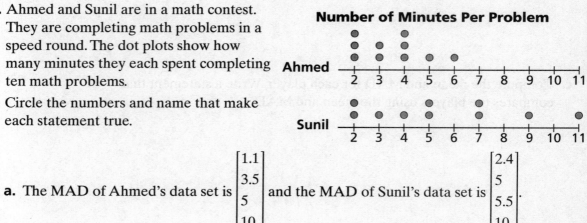

Number of Minutes Per Problem

a. The MAD of Ahmed's data set is $\begin{bmatrix} 1.1 \\ 3.5 \\ 5 \\ 10 \end{bmatrix}$ and the MAD of Sunil's data set is $\begin{bmatrix} 2.4 \\ 5 \\ 5.5 \\ 10 \end{bmatrix}$.

b. When comparing the distributions, the data vary least from the mean in $\begin{bmatrix} \text{Ahmed's} \\ \text{Sunil's} \end{bmatrix}$ data set.

Additional Practice

For Exercises 1–3, use the information below.

Pete plays quarterback on his school's football team. He records the length of each pass in yards in the table below.

Length of Passes (yd)

14	42	36	51	12	8
19	14	12	27	18	19
4	12	18	13	21	24
21	6	16	14	9	6
11	6	12	9	8	5

1. a. Draw a box-and-whisker plot to display the data.

b. Which whisker is longer? Why?

c. What information does the median give about the distances Pete threw?

d. Find the mean of the distances. Compare the mean and the median distances. What does this comparison tell you about the shape of the distribution?

Additional Practice (continued)

Length of Passes (yd)

14	42	36	51	12	8
19	14	12	27	18	19
4	12	18	13	21	24
21	6	16	14	9	6
11	6	12	9	8	5

2. a. Draw a histogram showing the distribution of the data. Use an interval size of 10 yards.

b. How many passes did Pete complete that were at least 10 yards long, but less than 20 yards long? Explain how you can use the histogram to find your answer.

c. How many passes did Pete complete that were 30 yards or longer? Explain how you can use the histogram to find your answer.

d. In what interval of the histogram does the median fall? How is this possible?

Additional Practice (continued)

3. a. Compare the shape of the histogram in Exercise 2 to the shape of the box plot in Exercise 1.

b. How does the height of the first bars in the histogram relate to the length of the left-hand whisker in the box plot?

c. How does the histogram help you understand the length of the right-hand whisker in the box plot?

d. Can you find the mean of the data using the histogram? Can you find the mean of the data using the box-and-whisker plot? Explain your answer.

e. Can you find the number of data values using the histogram? Can you find the number of data values using the box-and-whisker plot? Explain your answers.

Additional Practice (continued)

For Exercises 4 and 5, use the information below.

Mr. Keeler's class and Mrs. Booth's class competed in a push-up contest. The tables below show the data from each class.

Mr. Keeler's Class

Gender	Number of Push-ups
G	6
B	9
G	10
B	11
G	12
B	13
G	14
B	15
G	15
G	16
B	17
G	18
B	19
G	20
G	20
G	21
B	22
G	24
B	25
G	30

Mrs. Booth's Class

Gender	Number of Push-ups
G	6
B	10
B	13
G	14
G	14
G	16
G	18
B	20
G	21
B	21
B	21
B	24
B	24
G	25
B	26
B	27
B	29
G	30
G	35
B	35

4. Draw two box plots to compare the boys in Mr. Keeler's class to the boys in Mrs. Booth's class. From which class did the boys do better? Explain your reasoning.

Additional Practice (continued)

Mr. Keeler's Class

Gender	Number of Push-ups
G	6
B	9
G	10
B	11
G	12
B	13
G	14
B	15
G	15
G	16
B	17
G	18
B	19
G	20
G	20
G	21
B	22
G	24
B	25
G	30

Mrs. Booth's Class

Gender	Number of Push-ups
G	6
B	10
B	13
G	14
G	14
G	16
G	18
B	20
G	21
B	21
B	21
B	24
B	24
G	25
B	26
B	27
B	29
G	30
G	35
B	35

5. a. Make a box plot that shows the data for all of the girls in Mr. Keeler's and Mrs. Booth's classes combined. Make a box plot that shows the data for all of the boys in Mr. Keeler's and Mrs. Booth's classes combined.

Additional Practice (continued)

b. Compare the box plots in part (a). Who did better, the boys or the girls? Explain your reasoning.

c. Does that data for the girls include outliers? Does the data for the boys include outliers? Explain your reasoning.

d. Consider what you know about the outliers in the data. Does this change your answer to question (b)? Explain.

Additional Practice (continued)

6. Kelly gives each of her friends the same 100-piece puzzle. She displays the number of minutes it takes each friend to complete the puzzle in the graphs below.

Graph A

Graph B

a. What title and axis labels would be appropriate for Graph A? For Graph B?

b. i. Which friend completed the puzzle in the least amount of time? Which friend took the most time to complete the puzzle? What were their times?

   ii. Which graph did you use to find your answers for part i? Why?

c. Which graph can you use to find the typical length of time it takes to complete the puzzle? What is the typical length of time? Explain your reasoning.

d. If you were given only Graph A, would you have enough information to draw Graph B? Explain your reasoning.

e. If you were given only Graph B, would you have enough information to draw Graph A? Explain your reasoning.

Additional Practice: Digital Assessments

7. The box plot represents the number of Additional Practice points Carla earned last month for 10 different assignments.

Additional Practice Points

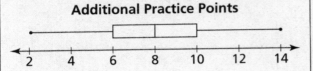

Use the tiles provided to complete the statements.

| 6 | 8 | 10 | 12 | 14 |

a. The range of the data is ☐.

b. The median number of Additional

Practice points earned is ☐.

8. Andreas recorded the daily temperature for several days. The box plot represents his data.

Daily Average Temperature (°C)

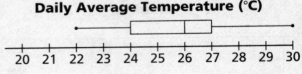

Which statements describe the data?
Select all that apply.

☐ The median temperature was 26°C.

☐ The range of temperatures is 3 degrees.

☐ The box plot cannot be used to find the mean temperature.

☐ The box plot can be used to find the mode of the data set.

9. The histogram shows the number of hours Kenya's friends spent exercising last month.

Circle the numbers that make each statement true.

a. Kenya collected data about exercising

from $\begin{bmatrix} 6 \\ 13 \\ 20 \\ 25 \end{bmatrix}$ friends.

b. A total of 4 friends spent between $\begin{bmatrix} 0 & \text{and} & 5 \\ 5 & \text{and} & 10 \\ 10 & \text{and} & 15 \\ 15 & \text{and} & 20 \end{bmatrix}$ hours exercising.

c. A total of $\begin{bmatrix} 2 \\ 4 \\ 6 \\ 10 \end{bmatrix}$ friends spent between 5 and 15 hours exercising.

Exercise Data

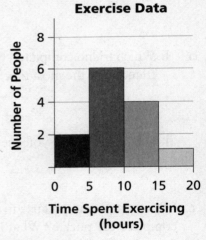

Number of People

Time Spent Exercising (hours)

Skill: Quartiles, Interquartiles, and Ranges

For each data set, find the quartiles, IQR, and the range.

1. 50, 60, 55, 70, 30, 50, 25, 90, 45

$Q_1 =$

$Q_2 =$

$Q_3 =$

IQR =

Range =

2. 30, 25, 15, 20, 20, 25, 35, 40, 30, 15, 25

$Q_1 =$

$Q_2 =$

$Q_3 =$

IQR =

Range =

3. 85, 70, 50, 65, 90, 80, 75, 80, 90, 95, 65, 80

$Q_1 =$

$Q_2 =$

$Q_3 =$

IQR =

Range =

4. 40, 70, 80, 65, 75, 85, 90, 85, 60, 55

$Q_1 =$

$Q_2 =$

$Q_3 =$

IQR =

Range =